Embracing the New Era

Creative Paths ^{TM}

First edition, published 2010

In the new era, creativity and innovation are the cornerstones of organizational and individual success. **Creative Paths** has the mission of helping people create environments where individuals and teams can achieve their creative potential. Through workshops and custom programs Creative Paths unlocks the creativity and innovativeness within individuals and businesses.

www.creativepaths.org

ISBN 1452848289

EAN-13 9781452848280

rev i

Embracing the New Era

Managing oneself & others in the era of creativity

André P. Walton, Ph.D.

Creative Paths™

Acknowledgements

In some respects all those around you contribute to the publication of a book. Your friends tolerate your long periods of absence from their social circles, distractedness when you do spend time with them, and your frustration when things go more slowly than you would like. So thank you to all my friends for your tolerance during the writing and publishing of this volume!

Particularly, though, thank you Robin Walton (my wife and friend), for your prolonged support and tolerance during this demanding process. Thank you also for your suggestions regarding the cover design as well as editorial content.

Many thanks also to a good friend, and one of my editors in a previous life as a journalist, Mike Dance, for his diligent proofreading and suggestions. This book definitely reads better as a result of them. Thank you Gordon Railton (world-class photographer, friend and fellow musician) for letting me use your superb solar panel shot on the cover, and to Ron Isarin for his shot of me on the back cover.

The seeds were sown regarding some of the concepts in this book, including the group affiliation model of creativity, while I was studying at the University of Nevada, Reno. I want to offer special thanks to my friend and PhD supervisor, Dr. Markus Kemmelmeier for his tutelage and unabating patience and support during my research and studies.

Finally, a big thank you to my mother, Christiane, for being a continual reminder throughout my life that *it's OK to be creative!*

Contents

Introduction

'Innovation is the specific instrument of entrepreneurship. The act that endows resources with a new capacity to create wealth.'

Peter Drucker

In the wake of World War II, in the early days of 'management-as-a-science', the words *management* and *creativity* were seldom used in the same sentence. Management was considered a skill based on sound scientific principles whereby decisions could be made deductively in the knowledge that certain choices would be 'right' and others 'wrong'. Creativity was considered the domain of a few select individuals who required special treatment and who worked in mysterious and often unpredictable ways.

That era of management research, theory development, and practice continued unabated based on solid capitalistic principles: Shareholder interests are paramount; expansion is sacrosanct; 'assets' include anything you paid hard cash for (but certainly not your human resources); the primary (if not sole) duty of employees is to obey management directives; any publicity is good publicity; the word 'community' is equivalent to 'customer'. This management model went largely untested until recently.

Most of these management icons have started to show signs of serious erosion. The 1984 Bhopal disaster sent the Union Carbide Corporation tumbling from the 6th largest company in the World to no. 27 (based on capitalization) and the business community started to realize that it had to start taking its public image seriously. In my youth if you went to a job interview you were probably preoccupied with thoughts such as 'what is it they are going to want me to say' or 'what is the *right* answer to that question?' Now prospective employees are much more proactive and demand answers to their own questions such as 'is this a company I am going to be proud to have worked for or are its ethics such that I am going to try and eradicate it from my CV at some time in the future?' or 'is this job the best way to get to where I want to be in my life and my career?'

In almost every area the old models are breaking down, or being challenged or changed. The financial turmoil of the first decade of the 21st century has been a serious test of management decision making practices. Take the days, weeks and months immediately following the 9/11 terrorist strikes. Knee jerk reactions took over from rational decision making in several critical industries, particularly the airlines. Nearly all major US carriers cut staffing levels, routes and flights, sometimes taking advantage of the opportunity to renegotiate union contracts. All this before there were any data regarding how the attacks would impact passenger demand. One exception in the industry was Southwest Airlines. Just three days after 9/11 Southwest announced that it would keep all of its employees, not cut any routes or flights, *and* start a $180 million profit sharing scheme. It is, of course, possible that all the other airlines took their decisions from a rational base also and just came up with different answers. But the fact is that the decisions made by Southwest have consistently prepared them well for the future compared to their competition.

This kind of clear headed, confident decision making is rare. Even when managers verbalize what they feel are the right choices, the end result is often very different. In a 2010 survey (Euchner, 2010) that included questions to technology leaders, two priorities were verbalized as being of high priority: "growing the business through innovation" and "accelerating the innovation process." Despite these promising responses, over 50% of surveyed companies anticipated staff cuts in research and development (r & d), and over 60% reported that their firms were already focusing r & d resources on shorter-term goals.

Some of the turbulence that individuals, businesses, even nations, have been facing came with some degree of warning and some did not. In a sense it might be compared to sailing into a heavy storm, possibly a hurricane. You have no idea what the experience is going to be like but for sure it will be a) different and b) ugly for some. You are unlikely to outrun a hurricane so you face two choices: drop the sails, go below and 'batten down the hatches'; or, shackle yourself to a lifeline and sail through it, possibly gaining some advantage from the high winds.

Knee-jerk decisions to cut employees, reduce product range, downsize, and cut r & d investment, represent the first approach – the head-under-the-bedclothes run-for-cover 'solution'. The second approach is an open admission that turbulence has within it opportunities. They may not be the same opportunities that are apparent in buoyant, expansive times but they are opportunities nonetheless. Finding and acting on these opportunities requires imaginative and creative decision making. That is what this book is about.

Specifically, I argue that it behooves you to make decisions in a creative way no matter what the economic and social environment, but in turbulent times this becomes crucial. In other words, the business world is recognizing that we need a new way of running businesses, and I am saying that creativity is a critical component of that.

One conclusion that is reached early in this book is that everyone has the potential to be creative. This has important implications for corporate structure and decision making. Creativity is not just the arena of a small number of 'special' people. The enlightened organization of the future will tap into this resource *in every employee, as well as other stakeholders*. Ideas come from customers, employees (who are also consumers), the community, and advisors. It is only when all these resources have been tapped that we can say our organization is optimized from an idea generation perspective; a perspective that will be increasingly critical to survival.

The game does not end there, of course, ideas need to be germinated and nurtured. Just as generating creative ideas requires the knowledge that 'it is OK to make mistakes' so turning ideas into innovations also requires a sympathetic environment; one that is shaped by communication, leadership style, individual motivation and team work. Once these things are all in place we have a chance of being competitive in the new era ... the era of creativity!

Chapter 1 – Towards the new era

'I think the human race made a big mistake at the beginning of the industrial revolution, we leaped for the mechanical things, people need the use of their hands to feel creative.'

André Norton

Every era has its 'currency'. There is always some resource that differentiates those that have it from those that don't. Before the industrial revolution, when agriculture was the predominant industry, labor was a critical resource. Large families were, of course, a generous source of almost-free labor. The produce generated by an adult dramatically outweighs the resources necessary to support him or her (in the days before credit cards, cell phones and BMWs, anyhow), so the more people in the farming family … the greater the wealth. Land is also necessary to facilitate agricultural growth but in North America homesteading[1] helped provide that resource at little or no cost (making it a non-differentiating resource). Elsewhere there were some similar schemes, and marriage sometimes provided a way for farming families to combine and gain the advantages of size.

As the industrial revolution started to have its swift and dramatic impact on Europe and North America, so the resources that were critical for success began to change. Railways, printing presses and manufacturing equipment have never come cheap and customers' enthusiasm for new products has always been difficult to prejudge. So, lots of cash and plenty of nerve were what you needed if you were planning to be at the top of the industrial heap. Lower down the corporate totem pole, however, industrialization generated a demand for a new resource: an educated middle management class. Previously there had been little call for this 'layer' in the organizational structure. Larger farms had a need for delegation of human resource tasks and slave owners had often employed a level of insulation

---

[1] The **Homestead Act** of 1862 was a US federal law that gave an applicant freehold title up to 160 acres of undeveloped land outside of the original 13 colonies. In 1909, a major update called the Enlarged Homestead Act was passed, targeting land suitable for dryland farming and increasing the number of acres to 320. In 1916, the Stock-Raising Homestead Act targeted settlers seeking 640 acres (260 ha) of public land for ranching purposes.

between themselves and their 'workforce' but the middle management that was spawned by the industrial revolution was different: It required education.

In other words, out of dozens or hundreds of people on the shop floor, if you were the one who could read, add and subtract competently those skills may have differentiated you from the others and enabled you to change your shirt from blue collar to white. Education, then, was the differentiating resource, and, to some extent, it still is. But things are changing. Although education is still a necessary requirement for landing a decent job in management it is not as much of a differentiator as it was. Just a few decades ago a college degree meant a good job. A Bachelor's degree from a *good* college meant a *great* job. Gradually a Master's degree took over as the requirement for a good management job (in the US anyway) and a PhD … well, you get the message. While college credentials are still necessary, so is something else. In other words, if everyone showing up for an interview has a bachelor's degree; it is no longer a differentiator. So, what is the new differentiator?

Historical background – Emotional Intelligence (EI)

Research on emotional intelligence began as early as the 1930s with Thorndike, Stein and Wechsler. (In 1920, E. L. Thorndike used the term *social intelligence* to describe the skill of understanding and managing other people (Thorndike, 1920)). David Wechsler considered intelligence in a rather different way than we do today, and thought of it as the "… capacity of the individual to act purposefully, to think rationally, and to deal effectively with his environment" (Wechsler, 1958). He also believed that we couldn't measure intelligence accurately "…until our tests also include some measures of the non-intellective factors" (Wechsler, 1941). This early work raised little interest until Howard Gardner wrote about intrapersonal and interpersonal intelligence, which he considered as important as the type of intelligence measured by IQ tests (Gardner, 1983).

Two different models of EI have been suggested. In one, EI is conceptualized as an ability or skill (Mayer & Salovey, 1997) or as a personality trait comprising cognitive, motivational, and affective factors (Petrides, Pita, & Kokkinaki, 2007).

The publication of Daniel Goleman's best-selling book *Emotional Intelligence: Why It Can Matter More Than IQ* saw the term *Emotional Intelligence* enter popular usage.

Daniel Goleman tried to put his finger on that extra ingredient in his books *Emotional Intelligence: Why It Can Matter More Than IQ,* and, *Working with Emotional Intelligence.* He describes EI as the ability to recognize our own and others' feelings, to motivate ourselves and to manage emotions well in ourselves and in our relationships. However, beneficial though the notion of EI may be, it is confusing, difficult to measure, and has not proved as useful as many originally anticipated. There are fundamental questions asked of EI that do not get satisfactory answers; such as: Can it be taught? What differentiates it from IQ? In fact, what really is it? (i.e. is it a clearly definable construct?) Can we measure it in any kind of useful, consistent and valid way? Also, there has always been an underlying suspicion that EI may end up being used primarily as a measureable factor that makes it easier for human resource managers to pick the best potential managers from a waiting room full of applicants; that is, after all, what a differentiator is. But, if we are going to make employment choices based on criteria such as EI then we had better have total confidence in its validity as a useful and definable construct, and not everyone does. So we shall have to look elsewhere for our differentiator.

Creativity as the new differentiator

"Creative thinking may mean simply the realization that there's no particular virtue in doing things the way they have always been done"

Rudolf Flesch

As I will discuss in later chapters, management *is* decision making and the new climate in which business operates demands creative management, and, therefore, creative decision making. But we need creativity for other purposes than making conventional management decisions. We need it throughout whole organizations for the purpose of generating innovative products and processes and because employees are demanding a more satisfying work environment. This includes the freedom to express their individuality and to feel that their lives can be influenced by the generation of creative ideas. The expression of individuality and job satisfaction go hand-in-hand. From an organizational perspective, in the era of global competition it is innovative products and innovative ways of marketing them that will differentiate successful businesses from those that are less successful. Increasingly people are realizing that every member of an organization has a role to play in the innovative process. Employees are not just workers; they are consumers, observers and, potentially, idea generators.

'In the August 1, 2005 issue, *Business Week* magazine reported that due to the emergence of low cost economies of Eastern Europe and Asia as the preferred locations for sourcing knowledge related activities (such as digitized analytic work and manufacturing), the focus of U.S. corporations is shifting from the knowledge economy to what is being referred to as the creativity economy. As a result of the increasing commoditization of knowledge, the creativity economy represents a change in paradigm – where the focus of competition will be on creativity, imagination and innovation. Leading through innovation in a creativity economy appears to be the only way (at least for the moment) that U.S. corporations and western corporations as a whole can gain and sustain competitive advantage. In a survey of over 900 senior executives by Boston Consulting Group Inc, innovation was identified as key to driving top-line revenue.'

(Oke, Munshi, & Walumbwa, 2009)

I am not suggesting that everyone is equally creative. People are not *equally* anything else so the notion that we are all the same regarding creative potential is likely to be nonsense. However, for an organization to attract and keep highly creative people it must develop an environment that nurtures creativity and that feels like an attractive place for creative people to work in. In the 'old way of doing things' the importance of creativity was recognized to some extent and creative people were treated in a special way because of it. When I worked in an electronics r & d department, we worked in a small building separate from the main factory and office complex. We worked different hours, we didn't have to punch in and out, and we were heartily resented by the test and maintenance engineers and other factory workers. It simply wasn't a comfortable position to be in. This separatist strategy did not encourage creativity from general employees (who were probably no less creative than the r & d team), or from the r & d engineers; on the contrary, it actively discouraged it.

The new model, then, has to be quite different. We have to generate a formula to create environments that support creativity in every way and from all organizational strata. Those environments have to be so committed to creativity that they feel comfortable for those people who are especially creative and they should also encourage ideas from those who may not have job descriptions relating to creativity or innovation.

But how do we know that creativity is becoming the new differentiator?

Consider the following: When agricultural workers left their farms *en masse* to walk the gold-paved streets and join the industrial revolution, Europe and North America were lucky. The jobs lost to the mechanization of agriculture were more than outstripped by jobs generated in the new industries of printing, large scale manufacture, the railroads, textiles, etc. All that was necessary was for people to be willing to relocate, which in the US, they often did.

Now we have a new kind of revolution on our hands: one that includes globalization. As with the mechanization of farming, many less challenging jobs in the US have moved location and many more will follow; this time, though, to foreign soil. Tax preparation, customer service, semiconductor design, telesales, computer programming, pharmaceutical manufacture, even the preparation of architectural drawings are being moved offshore for, often considerable, cost savings. For various reasons this trend may ebb and flow but since buying low and selling high is part of the capitalist model, there is no doubt 'outsourcing' is here to stay.

Table 1: Global Innovation Index 2008/2009 Overall Rankings

1. United States 5.28
2. Germany 4.99
3. Sweden 4.84
4. United Kingdom 4.82
5. Singapore 4.81
6. Korea, South 4.73
7. Switzerland 4.73
8. Denmark 4.69
9. Japan 4.65
10. Netherlands 4.64
11. Canada 4.63
12. Hong Kong 4.59
13. Finland 4.57
14. Norway 4.47
15. Austria 4.46
16. Taiwan 4.41

Now, unlike the heady and expansive days of the industrial revolution, there is no obvious yellow brick road to an alternative, burgeoning opportunity in the cities, in Silicon Valley, or anywhere else in the US or Europe for that matter. In other words there is no new industry waiting in the wings to absorb all those from the industrialized nations that no longer have jobs in telesales, tax prep and other outsourced occupations. Although the internet, like the offices and factories of the industrial revolution, is expanding rapidly, it does not seem to have the same capacity to create mass employment.

What we have to do as individuals, as organizations, as cities, even as nations, is to add value in ways that cannot (yet anyway) be outsourced. This means better exploiting what is already a major asset: our innovative skills.

As can be seen from Table 1 according to the Confederation of Indian Industry/INSTEAD Global Innovation Index, the US already leads the World in innovativeness. However, there are several indicators suggesting that the gap may be narrowing, and that in this and other critical areas the US may be losing ground.

In another Global Innovation Index, this time US-based, prepared by The Boston Consulting Group, the National Association of Manufacturers, and the Manufacturing Institute, the US ranked eighth among 110 countries in innovation leadership (Singapore topped the list, followed by South Korea and Switzerland.) The index is part of a broad research study that looked at both the business outcomes of innovation and governments' abilities to encourage and support innovation through public policy.

"America needs a bold innovation strategy," said National Association of Manufacturers' President, John Engler. "US manufacturing innovation leadership is at risk. We've fallen behind countries in East Asia and Europe. America cannot afford to lose its manufacturing innovation edge and the wealth and jobs that it generates throughout our economy" he said. Co-

---

Definition: **Innovation** from the author's perspective is the actualization of creativity. In other words it is turning an original idea into a novel and useful end product.

However, there are other definitions, including these from Joseph Schumpeter[1]:

- The introduction of a new good — that is one with which consumers are not yet familiar — or of a new quality of a good.
- The introduction of a new method of production, which need by no means be founded upon a discovery scientifically new, and can also exist in a new way of handling a commodity commercially.
- The opening of a new market; that is a market into which the particular branch of manufacture of the country in question has not previously entered, whether or not this market has existed before.
- The conquest of a new source of supply of raw materials or half-manufactured goods, again irrespective of whether this source already exists or whether it has first to be created.
- The carrying out of the new organization of any industry, like the creation of a monopoly position (for example through trustification) or the breaking up of a monopoly position.

[1] The Theory of Economic Development, 1934, Harvard University Press, Boston

author James P. Andrew had this to add regarding the report: "The emergence of challengers from rapidly developing economies such as India and China has transformed the playing field. With high-quality, inexpensive products flooding the market from every corner of the globe, competing on cost alone is a losing battle for most US-based manufacturers."

Finally, the Rand Foresight Report analyzes and projects the growth of 16 Technology Application areas, with a forecast out to 2020; their conclusions rank which nations are likely to apply and benefit from these technologies. They forecast that in 2020 the US will occupy the 6th/7th spot (tied with Israel), behind Canada, Germany, Australia, Japan, and South Korea.

Whether or not you can be convinced that there is cause for concern regarding the US capacity to maintain their innovative lead, from individual, corporate and public policy perspectives, maximizing creativity throughout the population has many positive aspects and no downside. From corporate as well as individual wellbeing perspectives it is increasingly vital to do so.

FAQ: Isn't *cash* a differentiator?

Of course, in a capitalist environment capital is always a necessary resource but it is not always the *differentiating* resource. While venture capital might be a bit tight right now, in general, since the latter part of the twentieth century if you had a good idea, the gift of the gab, sorry, ... a convincing business plan, and your request was not outrageous, then you could probably lay your hands on some seed money to become an entrepreneur. As evidence, according to Paul Reynolds[1], half of all US working males have a period of self-employment of one or more years at some time in their careers; one in four remaining self-employed for six or more years. The raising of significant amounts of capital is not, of course, a prerequisite for self-employment. However, the 120 US venture funds had over $15bn invested in new ventures in 2009, so many of America's entrepreneurs did require, and receive, cash. The point being that money is not currently a differentiator. As education has become commonplace so, to some extent, has venture capital. They are, in fact, both commonly available tools.

[1] entrepreneurship scholar and creator of the Global Entrepreneurship Monitor

---

Chapter 2 – The role of management

'Leadership: The art of getting someone else to do something you want done because he wants to do it.'

Dwight D. Eisenhower

Having discussed, in general terms, why creativity is the differentiator for individuals in the new era, let us now look at how creativity will be the differentiator at the organizational level. In other words how creativity needs to be applied and used in order to generate organizational advantage. Since any team is only as strong as its decision makers we first look at creativity in management, leadership and decision making.

This chapter is about an approach to managing which focuses on creativity. Before I expand on why this might have merit let us examine these two words and make sure we all understand the same thing by them.

What do we mean by *management*?

All organizations need guidance; the generation of a mission statement, perhaps, as well as the establishment and operationalization of short term and long term goals. These things define the difference between a group of people drifting in the same general direction, as a social club might, and a well-coordinated organization – whether corporate, public, non-profit, or religious, for instance. This guidance is often provided by a group of people some of whom are from within the organization – a committee, or board. The members of this group are all, to some degree, managers.

Often day-to-day management, in other words implementing decisions regarding the functioning of the organization, is conducted by one or more people, possibly including members of the board or committee. This person or these people have the responsibility for what we would recognize as the traditional tasks of management and they are often the decision makers regarding less major, day-to-day issues. They may also be responsible for human resource management of non-upper management personnel. These people are, of course, also managers.

> According to management guru Peter Drucker, the basic tasks of management are twofold: marketing and innovation.

Rarely, organizations share most or all of the day-to-day, or even the more major and long term, decision making among many or all of the members of the organization (e.g. the employees or associates). All of these employees are then, in some sense, managers.

Decision making as a structure

In many ways an organization's decision making protocol is a proxy for its structure. So, as most organizations are pyramidal in their power structure so they would be depicted as 'triangular' in their decision making structure (DMS). The aspect ratio, ('tallness' or 'flatness') of the triangle indicates how much of the decision making is delegated. In other words a tall thin triangle suggests a 'top-down' kind of DMS (with only a small percentage of associates participating in the decision making process). A 'flatter' triangle suggests that decision making is shared among a greater number of employees.

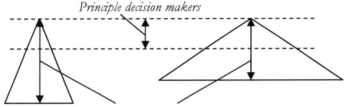

Principle decision makers

Those influenced by the decision makingprocesses

Less delegation in decision making   More delegation in decision making

Figure 1: Organizational decision making as described by either tall-thin or low-wide triangles.

A DMS doesn't have to be triangular; that shown in Figure 2 suggests delegation of decision making processes throughout upper management but with little of that responsibility shared by non-management employees.

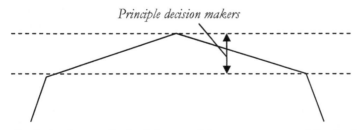

Principle decision makers

Figure 2: A 'polygonal' decision-making structure with decision-making capability biased towards the top.

We can expand the DMS to include lines of influence indicating the use of external personnel in decision making processes (who comprise the outer 'branches' of the decision making 'tree'). Many charitable organizations and organizations that represent professional membership (such as bar associations) make some of their decisions as a result of influences from members of an Advisory Board.

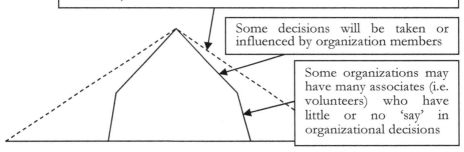

Decision-making as influenced by advisors, some of whom may not be 'full' members of the organization (employees or Board members)

Some decisions will be taken or influenced by organization members

Some organizations may have many associates (i.e. volunteers) who have little or no 'say' in organizational decisions

Figure 3. Dotted lines indicate 'decision influence' by advisors who are not from within the organization (i.e. they are not employees or Board members in the fiduciary sense).

A2.1 Think of the decision makers in a particular organization that you work for or are familiar with. Draw the DMS for this organization.

The 'advisory members' of the organization are not all 'board members' in the sense that they are listed on the Board of Directors (with the fiduciary obligations that that entails). They are often chosen for advisory board membership because of their particular standing in the community or in order to represent a point of view that is considered important to the organization; i.e. as stakeholders. These 'decision makers' often have decision-making capacity that is limited to their particular field or stakeholder interest and they may have none of the legal obligations that a Member of the Board would have.

My rather broad definition of *manager* may seem a bit of a stretch to some (for instance, the 'advisory board' is often at arm's length

A2.2 Choose a larger organization that you are familiar with (possibly the same one you focused on for A1.1) and list all the people who make up the decision making 'tree'. How many of these also make the day-to-day decisions for the organization?

from the day-to-day operation of the organization), but from one important perspective it makes sense. Ask yourself the question: Would it benefit the organization if this person or group of people enhanced their management skills? If the answer is 'yes' then they are probably managers.

East-West: From collectivism to individualism

Some North American and European manufacturing oriented organizations epitomize the kind of 'decision-making' shape shown in Figure 2 with a well defined distinction between 'management' and 'non-management'. However, the old Euro-U.S. model for manufacturing is not shared by all organizations worldwide. Japanese auto and electronics manufacturers tend to be more influenced in their decision making by all the vertical levels of the organization than their western counterparts. To some extent differences such as these may reflect differences in cultural norms, in particular, individualism/collectivism. In an individualist society it is acceptable, indeed, anticipated, that people will tend to put the interests of themselves and their families before the interests of 'the group'. Also, ambitions will tend to be individual in nature, in other words related to personal success rather than striving for the success of the group. In a collectivist environment, on the other hand, it is expected that individuals will put group interests before their own. It might be reasonable to suggest, then, that if the striving for and achievement of group goals is paramount then individuals within that group will be most empowered if decision making is a shared, (i.e. group) responsibility.

A2.3 List any reasons you can think of why individualist vs. collectivist cultural norms might influence the decision making structure of an organization.

Although not immune from problems, Toyota is a firm believer in the value of 'grass-roots creativity' and has made amazing inroads regarding innovation through 'communicating vertically' throughout the organization. Now this is not, I accept, identical to decision-making, but in a huge organization with a great disparity regarding decision-making skills and experience between upper and lower corporate levels, it is to be applauded that they made such inroads regarding 'total employee influence' which *will* impact the organization's ultimate fate even if it is only through an indirect route to corporate level decision-making.

There are three reasons for discussing decision making. The first is that, as mentioned before, management and decision making are intimately linked. In other words good and consistent decision making is a necessary skill for good management. The second reason is that creativity in management is all about *the way that decisions are made* in an organization.

The third reason is that even if decisions are made in a way that is conducive to creativity, there are plenty of organizational 'landmines' that can derail the implementation of new ideas and creative decisions. For example, there is little point in having a highly creative team deciding many of the day-to-day aspects of an organization's trajectory, if there is an unimaginative advisory board which has the last word regarding longer term goals. Not only will this be highly frustrating for the creative managers but innovative ideas may well get road blocked by the super-ordinate advisors. Unfortunately social entrepreneurial organizations (some non-profits, for instance) often tend to suffer from this predicament, with advisory board members acting as 'gatekeepers' for ideas that might be considered unconventional or for which they do not wish to take personal responsibility regarding the consequences.

Overall, then, if creativity and creative management are to have an influence over an organization's future, a commitment to creativity must permeate the whole organization from the style of its leader(s) and decision making practices at all levels, to inter- and intra- organizational communications.

So that provides us with a context for management and management decision making. Now, what do I mean by creativity……..?

Chapter 3 - Creativity & creative decision making

'All children are artists. The problem is
how to remain an artist once he grows up.'

Pablo Picasso

Being creative has several different meanings - from watercolor painting or playing the violin to brainstorming, writing software or inventing things. For me it means using specific cognitive practices that bring new ideas to bear on a problem, challenge or situation. Another way of saying it might be 'thinking or doing something that you have never done or thought before'.

> *Definition:*
> **Creativity** is
> 'Thinking or doing
> something in a
> way that you have
> never thought of
> or done it before'

Any of you think you are not creative? Think about this definition. It suggests, doesn't it, that we were all creative once? Between birth and sometime later (maybe as late as 9 years old if you were lucky), when socialization processes gained priority in defining how we think and act, weren't we all thinking and doing something new during most of our waking hours?

When I look at my young granddaughter, Emma, she seems intent on taking in and acting on all the new information she can absorb. She is perpetually thinking and doing things she has not *thought* or *done* before. As adults we tend to think of *Personal Growth* as something we gain by reading a text while writing in the associated workbook, or that we have to pay good money to attend a course on. As infants it was the natural thing for us to do. *Personal growth* is *creativity.* Just as many of us seem to lose the urge to be creative as we enter adulthood so perhaps we also lose personal growth as a natural process?

If we are to create an organizational environment that enhances the creativity of all its members we will be contending with extensive socialization processes that have already taken a creative individual into a non-creative socially-conforming space. Remember that being creative is all about doing things differently and finding ways of achieving an end result that has not been done that way before. Having a family, a school, an organization or a society where this kind of anarchism is encouraged makes life difficult! Much as we might enjoy the challenge of trying to create an organization where individuality rules, most parents, school principals, politicians and law makers and enforcers do not; they prefer a more orderly society to deal with. The result is a socialization process that is strongly demotivating to the expression of many forms of individuality; in other words, demotivating to creativity. Generally people are itching to get

A3.1 How and why might socialization processes be disruptive to creativity?

back to being creative and bringing creativity into their work and personal lives, but we have to appreciate that factors such as the fear of failure and reprimand run deep and it is likely they will temper their enthusiasm to create.

The fact that we are all inherently creative (if not equally so) has important implications for management. As mentioned earlier, traditional management structures tend to position creativity as something special that requires special people to do it and, sometimes, special working conditions to do it in. The design of a highly technical electronics control system, for instance, requires a skilled electronics engineer and there is little point in letting non-technical employees contribute to its design. So one can easily see how this traditional structure came about and has been perpetuated. But creativity in an organizational context is an 'applied practice'; it is a combination of many different elements including ideas, appropriate experience, motivation, communication skills and the ability to convince others, along with organizational factors such as leadership style.

Technology and human evolution

When we think of human evolution we often think of the staggering technological achievements by which we are surrounded. Whether or not you accept Darwin's Theory of Evolution (specifically, that as random genetic mutations occur within an organism's genetic code, the beneficial mutations are preserved because they aid survival) it does not directly explain how we have developed these sophisticated technologies (i.e. from Moorish water bucket pump to the solar cells on the cover of this book). There is something else required for this than the physical evolution of a powerful brain.

Water pumps and solar panels were not created by building endless numbers of random objects and then keeping those that aid survival. These inventions were the result of purposeful creative thought and innovation. From this perspective, then, human evolution *is* creativity.

If you are an architect you may not be a likely candidate to invent a new ultrasound imaging system; but since your work requires you to generate, use and manipulate images regularly, you *may* come up with a useful idea about imaging or displaying images. It might, however, require someone with specific skills to develop it past the idea stage.

A3.2 What kinds of questions or problems could be thrown open to all or most employees in your organization? Think of a specific decision or problem solution. How might the outcome have changed if it had been addressed organization-wide? Might it have had positive consequences?

The fact that everyone was once creative (and has the potential to be again) makes it worth considering whether a problem or question should be thrown open to all employees in an organization (and, possibly, other stakeholders, such as customers) rather than just a select few. Again, I am not saying that everyone is *equally* creative, simply that in the new era, creativity needs to come out of the closet and be integrated throughout all levels within and outside our organizations. It is no longer the domain of the ad. department or a few specialists in a padded cell with '*R & D*' written on the door.

At first glance my simple definition of creativity may not seem like any big deal but take a look at what you did today or yesterday and see if you can see any actions or thoughts that were different to any previous day? There were some, I am sure, but they may have seemed relatively unimportant and were swamped by the thoughts and decisions that simply mirrored similar ones made yesterday. That is only to be expected. After all, we make thousands or, possibly, tens of thousands of decisions daily, depending on the magnification with which you set your microscope, and most of them relate to repetitive actions and seem inconsequential.

Lazy daze – schemas

A3.3 Can you identify any decisions that you made today or recently that were similar but *not identical* to decisions or actions that you took some time back?

Our brains are inherently lazy. We prefer to use previously defined 'thought-paths' to solve recurring problems or make repetitive decisions. If we thought afresh each day about how to get dressed, how to eat our breakfast, how exactly and for how long we are going to brush our teeth, what route to take to work, and all the other minutiae of everyday life we wouldn't have the time or energy left to move ahead on any front – personal or professional. We generate pre-traveled patterns of thought, or schemas, which provide a level of efficiency that enables us to have the 'cognitive space' and energy to grow and do new things. The downside, of course, is that we get programmed to use these pre-trodden paths, *always*; even when it would benefit us to review all possible options before making a decision. Increasing the creativity in our lives and our decision making processes requires us to know when to override our schemas (and, possibly, those of others) and revisit a particular situation in a new light.

Definition: **A schema** (plural: either *schemata* or *schemas;* adjective: *schematic*) in psychology is:

- A mental structure that represents some aspect of the world.
- An organized pattern of thought or behavior.
- A cognitive framework focused on a specific theme that helps the organization of social information.

These schemas, by the way, can be influenced by the same things as the rest of our thinking and decision making processes. Culture and social norms, for instance, have been found to influence schemas, as have organizational norms, structure and leadership style.

A3.4 Can you identify any actions or decisions in your work that you make frequently, (almost) without thinking about it?

Trying to think of things that you do during the day that you act on using 'schemas' is difficult isn't it? Performing some actions has become so automated (i.e. schematic) that we don't focus on doing them; so it may even be difficult to remember the last time that we performed such an action. 'I must have had a cup of coffee today but I don't remember precisely when!'

Why is this important or relevant to management?

Once again: management *is* decision making; and creative management is using creativity and the generation of new ideas to make better decisions!

Often the decisions we make seem quite trivial. Sometimes, however, they are major in their potential consequences. Management decisions *always* have an impact on other people and the issue they are addressing is *always new!* In other words they are *never* exactly the same as decisions we have made before; in the time between a similar decision and now many things may have changed that influence the 'environment' of the decision. All decisions in the management setting, then, probably deserve to be viewed afresh – along with all the pertinent information. Management decisions made as the result of schemas, will not be creative and are unlikely to truly reflect the unique aspects of the current problem or challenge.

Making decisions creatively, then, is partly about knowing when to override schemas. This is not to say that we can't or shouldn't use past experience to guide our decision making, we should; but we should do so consciously and after considering all new material.

Decision-making for pro-action rather than re-action.

Many of the social institutions we are familiar with are essentially *reactive* in nature. Law-making, for instance, is generally a process wherein problems or questions emerge, and then laws are made *as a result*. These questions may be due to a new technology, such as stem cell research, or they may come from an event, such as 9/11, with the resultant 'war on terror', and, in the US, the Patriot Act and other legal consequences. Alternatively laws may be the result of legal precedent. Either way, with the exception of foundational socio-legal documents, such as the US Constitution, which try and be anticipatory in nature, legal decisions tend to follow case law, or federal or local governmental decisions, which themselves are reactions to individuals' perceptions of emerging problems.

We all work in different environments, so generalities will hit home for some but not for others. When considering how our working environments will change in the next few years there are some common factors that often

A3.5 Imagine your organization as if it were being 'managed for change'. In other words, if decisions were made *proactively* and were anticipatory in nature. No need to be critical of current management practices, rather, look carefully at your organization, group or department and ask yourself the following questions:

a. *What are the day-to-day and longer term goals of my organization/group/department?*
b. *What do we do on a day-to-day basis to achieve these goals?*
c. *Should these goals change to reflect the dynamic nature of our world? If so, how?*
d. *Looking at the day-to-day practices of my group or organization how should they change to reflect the revised goals? (Real goals and practices not some website/shareholder mission statement.)*

get built into decision-making processes, such as population expansion, economic inflation, crime rate predictions or interest and exchange rate changes. There are also many factors, however, that get consistently ignored. For instance, if I asked you: "Is the current economic (and to some extent, social) turbulence likely to continue, or have we seen the end of it for some considerable time?" What would your answer be?

Having asked that question of many people my guess is that you are likely to think that economic and social turbulence will be with us for some considerable time. If that is the case then ask yourself: 'What is my organization doing to prepare for this turbulent phase?' I could make a guess at what your answer might be to that also....... very little!

My point here is that when planning for the future we tend to think along the traditional lines of the old business models; in other words, using schemas that are based on what we have read, heard and been taught over the past few decades. We think in terms of expansion, of new products, length of lease agreements, interest and exchange rates, and, ...the bottom line. All these factors may be legitimate elements in our decision making processes but they don't directly help us with the one question that might be much more important than any other: "How do we prepare ourselves for the probable and dramatic future dips and peaks in our economic and social environment?"

> **A3.6 Can you think of some factors (such as population expansion) that might impact your business and work environment over the next few years?**

We need to introduce new parameters into our decision making and planning processes in order to better prepare for a turbulent future. These parameters will be different for each of us and the generation of ideas regarding what these are is an appropriate task for creative problem solving. It is also a crucial part of creative management.

Just to give you a few ideas, in a recent brainstorming session the team considered the idea of employee profit sharing as a part of salary, so that when the business is doing well so it can afford to pay more, and when it is doing less well the HR overhead reduces. This approach is not particularly novel but it shares the organizational risk between shareholders and employees. Wanting to extend this further, the team looked at other areas where this kind of approach might make the organization's overhead more flexible and sensitive to the economic climate. The group examined whether it might be feasible to consider leasing a building on that basis; in other words to enter into a rental agreement where some portion of the rent is fixed while the remainder is based on the business' revenues. Needless to say there were 'quashers' in the group who suggested straight off the bat that the idea was a non starter, but we continued to develop it anyhow. One of the team members was in real estate and agreed that although the unconventional nature of the idea might discourage some landlords, there are others who may have been looking at an empty building for way too long, that might be willing to give it a try. Of course there would be new hurdles to overcome, such as how to police the turnover of the business (and, thus, the amount of the variable portion of the rent), but if handled fairly and honestly the outcome *could* be positive for all concerned. The point here is that facing the likelihood that turbulence will persist enables us to come up with ideas before catastrophe strikes. This helps us make decisions on a more balanced basis rather than having only 'knee-jerk' schemas at our disposal. The safe option may sometimes be the best option, but it shouldn't be the *only* option considered.

൭Ცരു

'In the age of capital flows, only centers of innovation will be able to permanently capture the interest of investors.'

World Bank

The World Bank in its 'Advice to Nations' made the statement shown above. Strong words from an organization not traditionally known for its commitment to creativity! While the World Bank clearly has its focus on, well … money, it is highlighting *innovation* as being of critical importance to 'the interest of investors'. Whatever that phrase really means we can conjecture that WB is suggesting that money is going to follow innovation. And, innovation, as I hope you will be convinced by the end of this text, does not happen by accident; not consistently anyhow, as evidenced by the fact that most innovative organizations have a history of innovation. Even recognizing an innovative idea if it falls in your lap is inherently creative. However, consistently nurturing creativity within our organizations is really what we are after, and that requires conscious design, awareness and special leadership. Innovativeness doesn't just happen by good chance.

Chapter 4 – Creativity, groups and individuality

'The intuitive mind is a sacred gift and the rational mind is a
faithful servant. We have created a society that honors the
servant and has forgotten the gift.'

Albert Einstein

The previous chapters briefly outline some aspects of the relationship
between good management decision-making practices and creativity. To
examine this relationship further we have to look under the hood and try
and understand something about what creativity really is and why some
people may be more or less motivated to be creative than others.

When examining a human trait such as creativity it is helpful to think about
the different 'levels' at which humans can be studied. Until quite recently
creativity has been studied mostly at the individual level (Paulus & Nijstad,
2003). In other words individuals that society (or a researcher) has deemed
to be unusually creative are put under the psychological microscope and
examined. They may also be compared to other especially creative
individuals to see if there are commonalities between them. This approach
has not been very successful; which is why after 150 years or more of
research into creativity we know remarkably little about it!

Another level on which we can focus our microscopes is the societal level.
This does not deny creativity as an individual trait or phenomenon it just
works from the starting point that creative products with different
characteristics seem to emanate from different social groups. Therefore
societies may influence individuals regarding their creative motivations or
abilities. According to Social Identity
Theory (Tajfel, 1981; Tajfel & Turner,
1986), we are all composed of multiple
identities each of which is influenced by
our membership in, and identification
with, our ingroups. So this potential for
societal influence is not altogether
surprising. Indeed, creative products
from Eastern countries (which tend to be
more collectivist than their Western
counterparts) seem to be more
evolutionary in nature than Western
creations, which seem to be valued more

> *Definition:* To a psychologist
> a **group** is two or more
> people who interact with
> each other and share a
> common identity, interests
> or goals.
>
> **Ingroup** is simply a group
> to which you feel you
> belong, suggesting you feel
> loyalty and respect for the
> group and its members.

when they are revolutionary (Bhawuk, 2003). Viewing creativity at the societal level, then, may yield information regarding the underlying processes behind creative thinking.

I want to be clear that I believe creativity to be an individual phenomenon, in that the ideas that are so crucial to the generation of creative products come from individuals. This is true even if the individual is operating within a group or team. However, the relationship between the individual and their ingroups has an important role to play regarding the *motivation* to think in innovative ways.

At one level, then, this chapter discusses the individual and at another it deals with the group relationships that we all need and seek out. This chapter is controversial in the sense that my underlying theory, the group affiliation model of creativity, or GAM, while tested (Walton, 2006), is in its infancy and is somewhat cutting edge. It deals with the source of individual creativity, what motivates people to be creative and what demotivates them, but it does so within a group and ultimately, societal, context. The GAM has implications for personal growth, organizational innovativeness and, at the extreme, human evolution itself.

The same but different

Humans are a bundle of contradictions. We frequently hold contradictory thoughts in our heads and often try and rationalize them to seem less contradictory (reducing cognitive dissonance, as it is known). As well as holding contradictory opinions we are subject to contradictory drives, and I want to draw your attention to one pair of these in particular.

> **A4.1 Can you think of some situations when people seem to hold certain beliefs but then act in ways that appear to contradict them?**

> *Definition:* Having two or more thoughts or pieces of contradictory information causes the discomfort known as **cognitive dissonance**. According to cognitive dissonance theory we are motivated to reduce cognitive dissonance and the discomfort that goes with it by changing our attitudes, beliefs, or behaviors, or by justifying or rationalizing them.
>
> For instance, we may support a sports team that has just lost a match and justify their reduced stature by thinking or saying: "they may have lost but they played a much more sportsman-like game than the other bozos".

We all have a strong need for connection with others, for an affiliation with a group or groups. Psychologist Abraham Maslow suggested that this need is second only to the need for food and drink (Maslow, 1968), and Baumeister and Leary (1995) also considered group affiliation truly a need, comparable to basic physiological needs, rather than being just a desire. Military leaders throughout history have been aware of the strength of this drive and have recognized that depriving people of interaction with others provides a potent punishment in the form of solitary confinement. Most of us cannot tolerate being deprived of the company of others for long without suffering negative psychological and sometimes physical consequences. Individuals deprived of close social ties tend, for instance, to suffer from more health problems, have weaker immune systems, and a higher risk of mental illness and suicide (Joiner, 2005; Kiecolt-Glaser, 2001).

The other strong drive that we all have is to demonstrate our individuality and to have it recognized by others. The psychoanalyst, Otto Rank (1932/1989) saw this need to demonstrate individuality as the root of our desire for immortality (Becker, 1973). This desire, Rank believed, could be satisfied by distinguishing oneself from others during life in a way that would be remembered even after one's death. In other words, through creative action individuals anticipate that others will respect their uniqueness and afford them some degree of (at least, symbolic) immortality.

Our need to demonstrate uniqueness is also known by those who incarcerate others. Thus, prisoners' names are systematically replaced with numbers, and they are stripped of individuality in terms of clothing, diet, day-to-day activities, etc. in order to minimize their self esteem and overall psychological comfort.

These two drives are in opposition. In other words, when your connectedness with others is important to you, your individuality recedes in significance. When your individuality is salient, however, your group membership takes second place. To put it another way, when you are

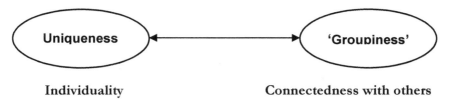

Individuality   Connectedness with others

Figure 4: The need for individuality vs. connection with the group
– the contradiction!

actively involved with an ingroup then it is your *similarity* with others that is of importance. When, however, you are focused on a task that involves your individuality (such as being creative), it is your *difference* from others that is pertinent.

The first of these points may be more obvious than the second. When we pursue an activity that involves something unique (it is creative, in fact), we focus on treading a cognitive path that has not been trodden by ourselves or others before. In other words, the very act of thinking or doing something that displays our individuality is inherently creative; and trying to be creative requires us to do something different and (at least conceptually) break away from our old thinking patterns and those of our group. In order, then, to demonstrate individuality (through creativity, for instance) we have to leave the comfort of group norms and break away on our own. This is the basis of the group affiliation model of creativity.

The creative is the place where no one else has ever been. You have to leave the city of your comfort and go into the wilderness of your intuition. What you'll discover will be wonderful. What you'll discover is yourself.

Alan Alda

> A4.2 Sometimes things happen that make our connection with others particularly important (the death of a friend or family member, for instance). Would that tend to encourage or discourage creativity according to the GAM?

It has been found that influences that tend to connect us with others (i.e. push us to the right hand end of the line in Figure 4) also tend to reduce our ability to think divergently (which is intimately linked to being creative). Simply watching someone, for instance, has been found to cause them to be less creative (Amabile, Goldfarb, & Brackfield, 1990). The GAM would suggest that this is because the mere presence of others focusing their attention on you makes the group salient. However, it is individuality and *escape* from others that is needed for the creative process. Also, when we feel threatened by a terrorist action (Arndt, Greenberg, & Cook, 2002), or even by the thought of imminent pain at the dentist (Arndt et al., 1999), we tend to gravitate towards one or more of our ingroups (or, in the extreme, towards complete strangers). In other words, connectedness with others becomes important to us. Following the terrorist attacks of 9/11 studies showed that students tended to feel more connected to their school or college; and families reported planning future vacations together and going to church more often (Moskalenko, McCauley, & Rozin, 2006). These actions demonstrate the need for stronger ingroup attachments when feeling threatened.

Another source of threat is competition. There are few organizations that do not operate under some kind of competition. Even non-profits are competing for donations, sometimes to the point where their future depends on it. How threat influences creativity is, therefore, an important question with a rather more complex set of answers than the above examples might suggest, and we will return to it in a later chapter. The point, for the moment, is that threat *does* have the potential to influence our motivation to be creative. It can either drive us towards connectedness with others, potentially reducing our creativity according to the GAM, or, it can motivate us to make extra efforts to address the challenge, potentially increasing our creative output. The precise outcome depends on other factors which we will discuss later.

Flying solo

Threat aside, when people are motivated to be particularly creative they often report the need or desire to get away from others. This may simply be that creating a good idea or product requires concentration and focus, and being alone is conducive to those things. On the other hand, the GAM does predict the need for departure from the group in order to create. In other words when we are trying to generate new ideas it is the uniqueness of our thoughts that needs to be salient and not the similarity with and comfort of our friends and similar others.

Let's look more closely now at how the GAM may help answer several questions and shortcomings that have arisen in organizational practices over the last few decades.

Problems with brainstorming

You may have been involved in brainstorming sessions at some time in your career. When Alex Osborn (1957) popularized brainstorming he anticipated that it would double the number of ideas that people would be able to generate in response to a problem, challenge or question. The fact that it did not, and that it actually reduced the number of ideas a group produced when compared with the number of ideas generated by the group's individuals on their own, was a source of frustration to him for the rest of his life.

In many ways brainstorming has been a major success in the field of management. It swept through the world of management consultancy (netting significant incomes and adding an exciting new item to consultant's menus), through management education and into most large organizations. Brainstorming makes people feel good. We tend to like working on projects with other people. Also, brainstorming is often wheeled out when there is a particular challenge or problem to address. Rolling up one's sleeves and 'buckling down' with others to 'get the job done' is very much a part of the Euro-American white-collar ethic, and a highly satisfying diversion from the normal day-to-day humdrum of many office jobs.

It comes, then, as a surprise to many people that brainstorming has this major shortcoming in that it is not an efficient catalyst of idea generation (ideation). Specifically, (and well established), if half a dozen individuals sit *by themselves* and think up ideas relating to the solution of a particular problem they will tend to come up with more ideas, when summed, than the same six people brainstorming together (in other words, sitting around the same table and thinking up ideas as a group) (Paulus et al., 1993).

A4.3 Using the GAM, can you suggest why the group-oriented process of brainstorming might generate fewer ideas than individuals working alone?

This book is not about brainstorming so I will not go into a detailed description of all the theories about why this shortcoming exists. Briefly, however, Alex Osborn and others, (see for instance: Diehl & Stroebe, 1987) suggested many processes that might come to play to cause the reduced efficiency of brainstorming compared with Alex's expectations (or with individual ideation). These include: 'freeloading' whereby group members 'sit back' on the basis that others 'seem to be doing great without them'; some members being more forceful than others and intimidating those more timid; those on the team having more power within the organization than others and therefore causing team members to acquiesce when they would otherwise come up with controversial ideas; 'groupthink' whereby a desire to avoid being seen as foolish, or a desire to avoid embarrassing or angering other members of the group, causes individuals to keep quiet rather than voice their opinions or introduce their ideas.

Even when brainstorming configurations and protocols have been designed to address all the above potential inefficiencies, brainstorming's ideation shortfall still persists! Considering that brainstorming is generally considered a critical part of creative problem solving and an important tool in the organizational decision making arsenal this is a major shortcoming.

Another explanation, based on the GAM, for brainstorming's shortfall is that, by its very nature, brainstorming is perceived as a group activity. Any group activity sends the individual racing towards the right (Connectedness) end of our Individuality/Connectedness continuum (remember that just the presence of another person has been found to reduce creativity). In other words, whereas the fundamentally creative process of idea generation requires us to be at the Individuality end of the map, this is in opposition to the 'group' format in which brainstorming is generally conducted. There are ways that this contradiction might be mitigated, which I will discuss later, but, fundamentally, the process of ideation is an individual one and the use of groups to do it is antithetical and counterproductive.

Team building

For several decades 'team building' has been a management buzz word, and for good reasons. Working in groups and feeling part of a team satisfies the need for connectedness that Maslow describes. Also, working in a team often affords more varied tasks than individuals are called upon to tackle individually.

Years ago Volvo broke away from the industry standard car construction practices that date back to Henry Ford, whereby each worker has a specific task, bolting cylinder heads onto cylinder blocks, for instance. The partly assembled car wends its way past each worker and gradually gets completed. Instead, Volvo established small teams of people to partially build cars. Instead of just tightening cylinder head nuts all day that same worker may now assemble a significant part of the engine, and maybe other parts of the car also. This led to increased job satisfaction and other positive attributes.

> A4.4 Take a looking at an organization with which you are familiar, are any of the organizational goals accomplished by teams? Are teams used for idea generation or creative purposes?

Unfortunately what embracing team building did *not* do was increase organizational creativity. In fact there is some evidence that it may have had a detrimental effect in this regard. Once again, according to the GAM, having people work in teams pushes them away from the 'individuality/creativity' end of the spectrum and makes the group, or team, salient. In the case of Volvo the tasks to be accomplished did not directly require creativity – the design work had long ago been completed and innovation was not the goal. So, the use of teams was perceived as having no significant negative consequences and plenty of positive ones. Under the 'organizational model for the new era' we recognize that the use of teams discouraging the kind of 'grass-root' creativity that motivates every employee to be part of the innovative process *is* contrary to our goal of achieving the creative organization.

In the new model, then, we have to find ways to satisfy people's fundamental needs, such as working closely with others, while satisfying the other fundamental need (and our primary goal) of allowing individuality and stimulating innovative products and processes. To pursue one and not the other is to throw the baby out with the bath water.

Table 2 shows the results of Employee Suggestion Systems (ESSs) in place at several Japanese companies and a typical large US business. For the Japanese companies the goals for establishing the ESSs were all similar and amounted to: motivation, job satisfaction, and group interaction. Toyota employees produced, on average, one idea per week, and they were not alone in that. An average of several large U.S. businesses running

Table 2. The annual results of Employee Suggestion Systems in place in Japanese and US businesses

Company	no. of suggestions	no. of employees	no. of ideas per employee
Matsushita	6,446,935	81,000	79.6
Hitachi	3,618,014	57,051	63.4
Mazda	3,024,853	23,929	126.5
Toyota	2,648,710	55,578	47.6
Nissan	1,393,745	48,849	38.5
Canon	1,076,356	13,788	78.1
Fuji Electric	1,022,340	10,226	99.6
Tohoku Oki	734,044	881	833.2
JVC	728,529	15,000	48.6
Typical leading US corp	21,000	9,000	2.3

Japan Human Resources Association, 1988, *The Power of Suggestion* employee suggestion schemes shows employee 'idea productivity' to be about one idea every 5 months! It is important to note that, in general, employees get individually rewarded with money for their ideas when successfully implemented (which, by the way, is somewhat contrary to the general notion that extrinsic motivation always has a negative influence on creativity (Amabile, 1983)). Also, it is anticipated that the original idea is individually generated, even though its future development may be within a team context.

Tsang (2002) suggested that the use of, and motivation for, ESSs is compatible with *Kaizen*, a Japanese core value that strives for improvement. So, although we might expect the individualistic US business to be the greater generator of ideas, it falls way behind its Japanese counterparts, possibly because the way that the ESS is structured is in line with Japanese social norms. We have no data regarding the 'quality' or innovativeness of the ideas generated, but most of Toyota employee's ideas are not reported as part of the ESS until implemented (which suggests that they are generally of useful quality).

As well as the financial incentive for successful ideas, there may also be intrinsic incentives such as the reward of heading a team to pursue the idea further. Either way, although the overall working practices at Toyota are team oriented, and it was certainly not the intention of the ESS to disturb that, but there was explicit room for individual thought and action built into the ESS process. Similar kinds of things can be done to all team activities in order to allow a balance between the expression of individuality and the benefits of group activity.

To be clear, then, I am not bashing team building; far from it. As the figures show, teams and ideas can co-exist within the same organization – there is a time for each. Creative problem solving is such an important part of decision making processes in the organization of the future that it will get a chapter to itself. But, for now, be aware that there are several stages within the innovative process where the use of teams is appropriate – just not at the truly creative stage of idea generation.

The social context for creativity

This chapter discusses creativity within its social environment. The goal is not to paint the whole picture regarding the mechanisms involved in the creative process, we will work towards that later; rather, it is to show how the motivation to create is influenced by social context.

Some of our social context is reasonably stable for most of us. For instance, we are unlikely to make frequent and dramatic changes regarding our most influential ingroups. In other words these groups do not often change regarding their structure, membership or norms. Individual group members may change their characteristics, as when our family ages, and group membership may change as happens when colleagues leave our work environment and are replaced by others. But, generally, most of the more influential groups in our lives remain fairly stable.

> A4.5 Take a moment to list your ingroups and write down the last significant change to the group and when that happened. Do the groups you belong to stay fairly constant?

> A4.6 Can you think of events that have happened in your life that generated a need to be more closely connected to other ingroup members at work or at home?

Other aspects of our social context *are* subject to change, however; sometimes dramatically. Whether or not you were in Manhattan at the time, 9/11 probably had a significant impact on you and your ingroups. For Americans and non-Americans alike, our 'national membership' was threatened. For Americans there was a closer bond to other Americans; a bond that, for many, needed to be visually demonstrated by 'flying the flag' on car radio antennas or in front of our houses. For non-Americans national group membership may also have been made salient in a different way and for different reasons (those victims could have been *our* citizens), but it was made salient nonetheless.

Less instant and shocking than events such as 9/11, but indicative of instabilities in our social context, nonetheless, are events such as the current economic downturn. This has dramatically altered the landscape in which our organizations operate, with an increase in the influence of competition and other intra- or inter-corporate threats. Our own personal positions within our organizations might also become insecure because of layoffs or structural changes. Any kind of threat has the potential to influence our motivation to be creative in part because our relationships with our ingroups become salient and the group norms become more influential.

Group norms

An important way in which our ingroups can influence us is by the attitudes of other members to our behaviors and actions (Ajzen & Fishbein, 1980;

Fishbein, 1967; Fishbein & Ajzen, 1975). At the societal level differences between group norms can be very obvious. In some societies taking multiple wives is considered normal behavior and, indeed, it can be a sign of wealth – the more wives the more wealthy and prestigious the man. In US society, in common with many others, having multiple wives is not only frowned upon, it is outlawed.

> *Definition:* **Group Norms** are the rules that a group uses for establishing appropriate and inappropriate values, beliefs, attitudes and behaviors. These rules may be implicit or explicit and failure to follow them carries with it the threat of sanctions or, ultimately, exclusion from the group.

The power of social norms is not limited to obvious or extreme situations such as multiple wives, of course, it has influence in all areas of our lives. Sometimes norms operate in quite subtle ways, and sometimes we would rather choose to deny the influence of social norms altogether on the basis that it seems to erode our sense of individuality. We may resent any suggestion that we are merely an agglomerate of the norms of the groups to which we are attached. Nonetheless, the reality is that a significant amount, if not the majority, of what makes us '*us*' is to do with social norms. Sorry!

From a creativity perspective this means that we will tend to be as motivated to create as is socially acceptable. Where creativity is not valued it will tend to be discouraged and other activities will be encouraged in its place. Also, our social norms tend to discourage making mistakes, which discourages us from taking chances – at least when the consequences are visible to others. If you have any doubts regarding how creativity is viewed in our society (true to some degree for all contemporary societies) take a close look at education systems. Anywhere in the world you will see priority given to 'core subjects' such as math, reading, writing, and then science and technologies. Art, music, drama, creative writing tend to be of much lower priority (in other words, at the very end). That is not to say that there is not the potential for creativity in math and writing, or science and technology, of course there is, but only if the subject is taught in a way that suggests creativity to be an important component; which is not, I believe, generally the case.

From an organizational perspective, there are several factors regarding organizational norms that can help generate an environment that is conducive to creativity, and we will discuss these in greater detail later.

But briefly, organizations that explicitly support creativity and that generate environments in which people feel secure with the notion that it is OK to make mistakes, will tend to be more innovative than those that do not. Establishing and maintaining this kind of organizational norm sometimes requires quite major structural changes, as well as examination of the prevailing leadership style, management structure and communication conduits. Also, the extent to which individuals in the organization or group are 'reined in' by its norms depends to some extend on how closely connected they feel to it.

Group Identification

Not all the groups we belong to have an equally powerful influence over us. The extent to which we feel connected to a group, feel attracted to and admire other group members, and share behaviors common to the group, dictates the degree to which group norms influence our thoughts and behaviors (Jetten, Postmes, & McAuliffe, 2002). The quantification of group identification is not an exact science, particularly since we are often attached to groups of different structures, sizes and other characteristics, but we can probably list our group influences in some kind of order even if we cannot apply a scale. For instance, our relationship to our nation and to others of the same nationality has conceptual differences to our feelings towards our local chess club, amateur football team, church or family. They are, however, all examples of possible group memberships with the associated variable of group identification.

> **A4.7** Look at your list of ingroups from A4.5 and place them in some sort of order regarding their importance to you and the influence they have on you. Is there a wide or narrow spread of influence?

Definition:
Group Identification is the psychological attachment felt towards a group or its members. This attachment is thought to have three roots: cognitive (how we categorize ourselves, socially), affective (do we *like* other group members), and behavioral (our actions are influenced by those of other group members.

The relationship we have with our ingroups can be altered by external factors. For instance, threat tends to increase individuals' desire for connectedness with others (Branscombe et al., 1999; Branscombe & Wann, 1994; Branscombe, Wann, Noel, & Coleman, 1993). This translates to a higher level of group identification. Following a threat to our nation we may choose to forgo a visit to the chess club in favor of spending time with our family. This is partly because our identification with our family might be stronger than with the chess club, and partly because our social norms tend to suggest that under threat family membership is of a higher priority than most other group memberships. These social norms may be particularly salient following a threat to our nation. If our national ties are less strong we may feel less need to adhere to its social norms even after a national threat.

As an example of the relevance of these issues in a management context consider the following: There is an academic model called the *cosmopolitan-local latent role construct*. Broadly, 'local' individuals tend to identify with and feel committed to the organization where they work. 'Cosmopolitans', on the other hand, are committed to maintaining the skills and

> **A4.8** According to the GAM would strong group ties and high group identification be more or less conducive to creativity than weak ties and low group identification?

values of their profession (Gouldner, 1957) and will tend to have weaker ties to colleagues and the 'work group' compared to the local individual. In other words, cosmopolitans' identification with their work group is likely to be less compared with the local individual, even though their identification with the group that includes professionals in their field may be as strong or stronger. Whereas we may intuitively place high value on the loyalty of the local individual it may be the cosmopolitan that is more motivated to be creative (as a function of, or as indicated by, weaker group ties and lower identification with the work group).

From group norms and our feelings of attachment to our ingroups, to leadership style, competition and threat, there are powerful social and situational influences regarding our motivation to be creative both in and outside our work environment. Ultimately, however, it is the individual who generates ideas and makes the unusual connections that lead to innovation. The leaders of creative organizations need to address these issues, and more...

Chapter 5 - Creativity at the individual level

'You could know every bit of neurocircuitry in
somebody's head, and you would still not know
whether or not that person was creative'

Howard Gardner

Having examined some of the social influences on creativity it is important to be aware of individual psychological and even physiological factors that have come to light regarding individuals' tendencies to be creative.

The stages of creating

Before we examine these in detail let us take a brief look at what the process of being creative in an organizational context probably entails. Broadly, if we are trying to deliberately generate a new product or process we will probably follow these stages:

1. Establish a framework within which innovation can occur; i.e. what kind of process, product or problem are we trying to generate? Is it evolutionary or is it a dramatic departure from what we already do? What budgetary and time constraints are we working within?
2. Assemble ideas regarding what the challenge is and how it might be tackled. These ideas should come from as many sources as possible – customers, employees, feedback from trade shows, what the competition is doing, etc.
3. Choose which idea to pursue and design a 'who does what and with what expected outcome' kind of route map.
4. Follow the path with regular checks against the route map and re-evaluate or correct as necessary.

I am not suggesting that this is how people are creative *in general*. There is no doubt in my mind that when eminent painters, composers, even inventors created something that we now recognize as groundbreaking (even if it wasn't recognized as such at the time) they probably didn't follow this kind of path. In reality, people that often invent or are used to thinking and acting creatively short circuit the above process, or they may use a different paradigm entirely.

Once innovation becomes the norm in our organization the above steps may change character, and the process may become more like the creative process that painters or composers go through. However, starting from scratch in the innovating process the above steps, or variations on them, form the kind of path that we can take to identify and pursue a challenge creatively.

Deductive vs. intuitive thinking

At each of the above steps, with the possible exception of the last, there is room for both deductive and intuitive cognitive processes. In other words, in choosing the most appropriate way to identify or address the chosen challenge, intuition might guide you down a particular path. Alternatively, you might use a rational, logical thought process to simply eliminate certain options because it is apparent that they use resources to which you cannot readily gain access.

Logical and deductive processes are pretty easy to define. Our contemporary world is based on many logical relationships and deducing courses of action from available data is part of what we need to do in our everyday lives in order to avoid disaster and minimize problematic situations.

Intuition is altogether harder to put your finger on. To psychologists it is one extreme of Carl Jung's two dichotomous pairs of cognitive functions: the "rational" (judging) functions: *thinking* and *feeling*; and the "irrational" (perceiving) functions: *sensing* and *intuition*. From these were derived the four axes of the Myers-Briggs Type Indicator[2]: Extraversion/Introversion, Sensing/Intuition, Thinking/Feeling, Judgment/Perception.

The *thinking* end of Jung's thinking-feeling dimension refers to a preference for logical thought processes. The *feeling* end refers to the inclusion of compassion, relationship considerations and personal values when making decisions. Jung suggests that these two opposites reflect a *judging-perceiving* dichotomy, in other words those at the *thinking* end of the scale tend to *judge* and plan and those at the feeling end tend to *perceive* and be spontaneous (Dollinger, Palaskonis, & Pearson, 2004).

---

[2] The **Myers-Briggs Type Indicator** (MBTI) assessment is a psychometric questionnaire designed to measure people's psychological preferences regarding how they perceive the world and make decisions.

From a creativity perspective there may be some interesting parallels between Jung's dimensions and the GAM. At least in the contemporary west, when individuals are in a group context there are pressures to make decisions and act from the thinking/judging end of Jung's cognitive continuum. People say admiring things about those who are 'sensible' (i.e. logical, perhaps even dispassionate) in their decision making, and they frequently say not so admiring things about those who make seemingly impulsive decisions that are emotion-driven.

However, once we have escaped the gravity of our ingroups and their norms and are at the *individualist* end of the GAM continuum it may be feeling and intuition that lead us to connect ideas that are not logically related: leading us to think creatively, in other words. Indeed, this is exactly what Dollinger, Palaskonis and Pearson (2004) showed in their experiments revisiting some classic findings regarding the Myers Briggs Type Indicator's capability to predict creativity. Specifically, they found that creativity was most evident in intuitive-feeling types of individuals who, according to MBTI developers, learn best by imagining, and they need freedom to do things in their own creative ways (Myers, 1998, p. 37).

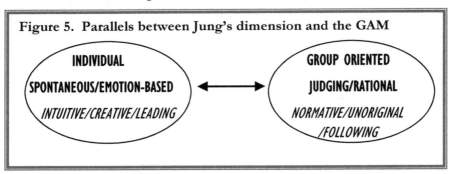

Figure 5. Parallels between Jung's dimension and the GAM

However, none of this really helps us understand what intuition really is. Formal definitions include: *the mind's immediate comprehension of something without reasoning;* or, *knowing something without prior knowledge or the use of reason;* neither of which really captures the importance of intuitive thought.

Back in 1994, Antonio Damasio conducted studies of patients with frontal lobe brain damage. He found that these people could generate accurate accounts of their experiences but, somehow, could not learn from them in a practical sense. From these studies he concluded that intuition is crucial to learning and is a vital link between our understanding and our actions.

A5.1 Think back to a major decision that you made (accepting a particular job or buying a house, for instance). See if you can assess how much of the decision was 'emotive' or intuitive, and how much was 'rational' (pros vs. cons) or deductive. Was it your deliberate intention to make the decision that way?

Personally, I believe we often think about things less logically than we like to admit. The same schemas that come into play regarding our decision making processes also influence all our thought patterns, and if something seems to work, why doubt it or over-analyze it? Imagine you have been designing aircraft engines or writing software all your working life (and perhaps you have!) and someone comes to you with a 'How to?' question to which they want your brief ideas. Your initial answer may draw more on your extensive experience of what worked in the past and what did not, than the use of logic or deductive reasoning regarding the current problem.

Sigmund Freud suggested that while everyday decisions can be made deductively, by weighing up the pros and cons, important decisions need to '… come from the unconscious, from somewhere within ourselves'. In laboratory experiments conducted by Wilson and Schooler (1991), students were asked to taste and grade various brands of strawberry jam. When their judgments were compared with those of experts, the students who made unguided assessments faired significantly better than those who were told they would have to explain the reasons for their ratings. The unguided judges probably used more intuitive cognitive processes than the other students who knew they would have to give a rational explanation for their choices. Also, in a follow up study, Schooler found that the students who knew they had to explain their decisions (and were probably therefore less intuitive) were less satisfied with their choices.

There is evidence, then, that the quality of decision making depends to some extent on the use of intuition. There is also evidence that this is particularly true of complex problems. Ap Dijksterhuis (2004) presented student participants with twelve pieces of information regarding four hypothetical apartments in Amsterdam. The information presented was such that one of the apartments clearly had more positive attributes than the others. Some participants had to make a decision immediately after being presented with the information, some participants had time to think about it, and a third group was distracted for a short while and then asked to rate the apartments. There was no difference between groups who had time to think about their choice and those who had to make a choice immediately. However, the ones who were distracted, and therefore had to make a rushed choice using unconscious thought processes, significantly outperformed other groups. In a further experiment it was found that the 'unconscious thought' decision makers seemed to form a more 'global' judgment that was based on more information than the conscious thinkers. This finding is in line with Wilson and others (e.g., Wilson et al., 1989; Wilson & Schooler, 1991) who showed that employing conscious thought processes tends to cause people to focus on just a few elements at the expense of other available information when making decisions.

I had a frustrating moment a while back with the Windows operating system (I know I am not alone, by the way!). While trying to retrieve files from my dead laptop the security protocol on my laptop's hard drive was preventing me recovering the data. I called an experienced hack-friend of mine who had the problem solved in 5 minutes, despite not having addressed the same problem ever before. "How did you know to go down that obscure (and undocumented) route?" I asked. "I don't know. It just seemed like that's the way those guys would have written it." He replied.

Intuition or not I was most grateful! Whether that example fits everyone's meaning of intuition, it illustrates that thinking processes can be brought into play in solving a problem or meeting a challenge that get the job done but do not fulfill the criteria for logical or deductive thought. For me, that's intuition.

Notice that in the above example of my dead laptop *skill, knowledge* and *experience* were necessary for the 'intuitive' problem solution. So, too, are they necessary for innovation. At each stage in the innovating process they play an important role. For instance, the more knowledgeable you are in a field the easier and more likely it is for you to identify challenges or problems that need addressing. Also, the better equipped you will be at judging which problem solving approach is most suitable. So, although those with skill, knowledge and experience will not necessarily be innovative, it is likely that innovative (i.e. creative and useful) ideas will come from those that do possess these three attributes.

Innovative ideas may also come from people who are particularly attentive to small quantities of information – clues. In an experiment designed to find the value of clues in people's problem solving abilities, Westcott (1968) made several clues available to participants who were given a problem to solve; they could use one or two clues or they could opt for more. Westcott's results can be illustrated using a 2 x 2 matrix.

There are two groups that emerged from Westcott's experiment; one did consistently well using very few clues, Westcott's *successful intuitives*; and another group did consistently badly with many clues (as many as they wanted), the *conservative failures*.

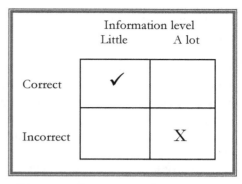

Figure 6. Westcott's *Successful intuitives* vs *Conservative failures*

Compared with the conservative failures, the successful intuitives tended to be unconventional, resisted being controlled by others, confident in their decisions, and they were self-sufficient and introverted. To me these attributes suggest the kind of individuality with looser ties to the group that you might expect from someone at the 'individuality' end of the GAM continuum.

Since intuition seems to play an important role in being creative, we would expect that creative people might share these attributes with Westcott's 'successful intuitives', which they do seem to. As well as the possession of skill, knowledge and experience, there are also other characteristics that have been identified as being associated with creativity.

Mentoring and Motivation

Although research into what highly creative individuals have in common has not given us very much useful insight into creative processes, two factors have consistently emerged, particularly from archival research examining biographical information about eminent writers, poets and other creative people. First, eminent creators seem often to have had a mentor; someone they respected that also provided guidance and support. There is no evidence, though, that this factor is unique to *creative* eminence, it might simply be a characteristic of *eminence*. Nonetheless, having a mentor probably serves three roles in supporting creativity. First, the mentor may help the individual persist in their creative quest through times when they might otherwise have quit. Second, and not unrelated, encouragement from the mentor probably 'balanced out' prevalent social norms disfavoring creativity. After all, if you are born into a family of musicians, writers or inventors you are likely to feel that it is OK to be one of these yourself (no matter what the norms outside the family). Mentors may also have provided some assistance in the area of skill development, since they often seem to have had skills in the same or a similar domain as the mentee.

The second factor that has frequently emerged as being common to eminent creators is motivation. Once again, there is no evidence that this is a trait unique to eminent creators, being eminent in most domains requires some degree of motivation and dedication doesn't it? There can be few eminent people who couldn't get out of bed in the morning whether or not they were eminent because of any creative accomplishment. Nonetheless, being *consistently* innovative undoubtedly requires persistence (i.e., patience and motivation), and our innovative organization must recognize the importance of this and not let impatience or short term thinking win the day!

The 'snowflake model'

There are other psychological individual-level traits of creative people that researchers have identified over the years, and they are probably best summarized in David Perkins' 'snowflake model of creativity' (Perkins, 1981). Perkins' six-sided model (hence the name) suggests that creative people have the following characteristics in common:

> 1. *A strong commitment to a personal aesthetic.* Creators have a high tolerance for complexity, disorganization, and asymmetry (this is now captured by the phrase 'tolerance for ambiguity'). They enjoy the challenge of struggling through chaos towards a resolution and synthesis.

> 2. *The ability to excel in finding problems.* Asking the right question can lead to discovery and creative challenges and solutions.

> 3. *Mental mobility.* Creative people find different perspectives and approaches to problems (that is what creativity is, after all). They also have a tendency to think in opposites, metaphors and analogies, and they challenge assumptions as a matter of course.

> *Definition:* A **high tolerance for ambiguity** is the ability to perceive ambiguity in information and behavior in an open-minded, non-threatened way, and has been shown to correlate with creativity (Kirton, 2004).

4. *A willingness to take risks and the ability to accept failure.* They learn from failures. By working at the edge of their competence, where the possibility of failure lurks, mental risk-takers are more likely to produce creative results.

5. Creative people not only *scrutinize and judge their ideas or projects, they also seek criticism.* Objectivity involves more than luck or talent; it means putting aside your ego, seeking advice from trusted colleagues, and testing your ideas.

6. The last trait is that of *inner motivation.* Creators are involved in an enterprise for its own sake, not for school grades or paychecks. Their catalysts are the enjoyment, satisfaction, and challenge of the work itself.

Some of these traits suggest that there is an element of anarchy in the creative process! Indeed, doing something differently from everyone else is a characteristic shared by both creators and anarchists. Also anarchists, almost by definition, are probably only loosely bonded to the social group about which they are being anarchistic. The GAM suggests this is a characteristic shared by those who are creative. The leadership style, then, for our innovative organization had better be able to cope with some degree of rebelliousness and *a*normal thoughts and actions.

Trait three, mental mobility, is somewhat vague but does touch on a key element in the creative process; one that tends now to be called lateral thinking[3]. Like intuition, mental mobility or lateral thinking are not deductive. Rather, they refer to the bringing together of ideas from different disciplines or experiences (domains) that are not obviously or rationally connected.

> In World War II a 'bouncing bomb' was used to bounce across water to a strategically important dam so as to avoid enemy torpedo nets. When British engineer (and somewhat of an anarchist, by the way), Barnes Wallis, invented the bomb he drew the idea from the way that pebbles can be skimmed across the surface of the sea.

---

[3] The phrase **Lateral thinking** was coined by Edward de Bono in 1967 in *New Think: The Use of Lateral Thinking*

Drawing on childhood experiences in the way that Barnes Wallis did is unlikely to be the result of a deductive approach to the problem. It results from the kind of lateral thinking that is sometimes described as being more akin to play than problem solving. This kind of mental agility or ability to connect disparate experiences and ideas is critical to the creative process, and is probably more prevalent in people whose cerebral hemispheres communicate well and often (good left-brain, right-brain communication).

Perkins' contention that "Creative people ... seek criticism" may or may not be true, but in terms of evaluation (not the same as seeking judgment, admittedly) influential psychologist, Carl Rogers[4], was quite clear in his belief that evaluation of a creative individual should be *self*-evaluation and not evaluation by others (Rogers, 1954). Rogers was also of the view that creative people were driven to be creative through the desire to fulfill their potential. In other words, he agreed with Perkins (trait 6) that the motivation to create is *intrinsic.*

There has been some debate regarding the relative importance of intrinsic versus extrinsic motivation. One school, headed by Teresa Amabile, believes that intrinsic motivation is conducive to creativity and extrinsic motivation is almost always detrimental (Amabile, 1983; Deci & Ryan, 1985). On the other hand there is some evidence that when a reward is offered that specifically relates to *creative* performance (rather than performance in general) creativity is enhanced (Eisenberger & Rhoades, 2001). There is some further evidence for this in Table 2 which shows the results of employee suggestion schemes, which involved individual (generally monetary) reward.

> A5.2 If you wanted to reward employees for being creative appropriately and without using money, how could you do it?
> Try and think of rewards that would positively reinforce creativity.

Historically it is the case that if extrinsic reward (i.e. money) had failed to encourage people to be creative we would be without many outstanding and unique works of art, music and architecture. For me the question should be: When financial or other extrinsic incentives succeed in encouraging creativity, why does this happen? In other words does the reward (i) demonstrate a social norm encouraging creativity and suggest to the creative individual that it is definitely 'OK to be creative'; (ii) leave the

---

[4] influential American psychologist and among the founders of the humanistic movement

creative individual free to create without the worry and distraction of where the next rent check is coming from; or (iii) simply satisfy a human greed for worldly wealth (or, a combination of all three). There are, as yet, no clear or conclusive answers to these rather basic questions.

Intelligence

You may have noticed that intelligence is not on the list of Perkins' prerequisites for creativity, and this is in keeping with the findings of other researchers. Attempts to study whether creative ability correlates in any way with intelligence have been fraught with problems including: how we measure creative ability or potential; how we measure intelligence (as opposed to the ability to do well at IQ tests); and, whether we can measure them both at the same time and in the same environment. The measurement of both IQ and creative ability or potential has been the subject of much debate. IQ measurement seems to have yielded the most stable results of the two; however, many researchers do not believe that we are always measuring what we think we are[5]. One problem with IQ measures from an archival research perspective is that the base line changes from year to year in order to keep the average score at one hundred[6]. In other words the same individual may rank differently from one year to another, not as a function of their individual aptitude at IQ tests but because of the aptitudes of everyone else with whom their score is ultimately compared. However, this problem may not be great considering the margin of error in such tests.

Despite the above problems and debate, the general view is that an above-average IQ is conducive to creative performance. However, above about 120, intelligence seems to add little to creative achievement. This has become known as the *threshold theory of intelligence and creativity* (Torrance, 1962; Yamamoto, 1964; Guilford, 1967). However, much of the research in this area has looked at creativity from an 'achievement' perspective, trying to establish whether a certain IQ level is associated with creative eminence (whether in math, architecture or some other field). Any relationship might have been more to do with *eminence* than creativity. Or, a relationship between creativity and IQ may have been due to the

---

[5] IQ scores have been shown to be associated with such factors as parental social status, and to a substantial degree, parental IQ. While the mechanisms by which IQ could be inherited have been investigated for nearly a century, controversy remains.

[6] The scoring of modern IQ tests such as the Wechsler Adult Intelligence Scale is based on a projection of the subject's measured rank on the Gaussian (bell) curve with a center value or average IQ of 100, and, generally, a standard deviation of 15.

association between skills in the particular field and innovation. In other words it may not have had anything to do with the ideation (creative) component of the innovative process, or the ability to think divergently, which has been associated with creativity (Torrance, 1974) and is often the basis of creativity measures.

Physical factors

Most books on creativity do not talk much about the possibility that there are physical characteristics or processes that an individual might possess or go through that may influence their ability to be creative. But there are three that I think are worth mentioning.

Sigmund Freud introduced the terms "primary process" and "secondary process" to describe different modes of cognitive functioning which are thought to lie at opposite ends of a continuum. Primary processes are un- or pre-conscious, unlimited by time constraints and volatile by nature. Dreaming and day-dreaming, where the mind wanders without much apparent direction, connecting ideas in a way that is difficult to remember or fathom, are primary process activities. On the other hand secondary processes have boundaries and direction and are conscious and reality-oriented. Certain psychotic states such as schizophrenia are thought to result from individuals being unable to control (or, sometimes even know) whether they are in primary or secondary processing mode. The maintenance of a healthy human psyche is thought to depend on the equilibrium between these two types of thought processes. Psychologically healthy people often drift from primary to secondary ends of this continuum without thought, but when we are under pressure (time constraints, for instance), we preferentially revert to secondary processing.

Kris (1952) suggested that creative people are better able to move between these two types of cognitive processing than are non-creative people. In particular, he believed creative people are better able to access primary cognitive processes. This, Kris suggested, is conducive to the type of non-logical connection of ideas that is what being creative is all about. This suggests that stressors such as a rigid timeframe are counterproductive from a creativity point of view since they tend to induce us to process information using secondary processing. On the other hand, after being creative we need secondary processes to get back to some kind of structured, logical thought in order to turn creative ideas into something useful (i.e. innovations).

46

Earlier I briefly discussed the importance of what Perkins called *mental mobility* which has common elements with what De Bono calls *lateral thinking*, I will call it simply *mental agility*. As suggested before, using creative processes to address a challenge uses mental agility and it brings to bear some degree of experience and skill. If Barnes Wallis had not been a highly experienced engineer he may not have recognized the feasibility of using a 'pebble skimming' technique (an idea possibly derived from primary processing) to send a bomb across the surface of water. He may also have had knowledge and experiences relating to materials and buoyancy, for instance, that guided him in his solution through secondary processes. This is related to the notion that I will discuss next that we need to employ both hemispheres of the brain in order to be innovative.

Broad generalizations are often made regarding certain functions, such as reasoning or language, being located in a specific cerebral hemisphere, whereas many important functions are distributed across both halves of the brain. However, if we look at the kinds of mental processes that are involved in innovation we find that both halves of the brain play vital, and different, roles. The left hemisphere is crucial for the deductive, reasoning part of challenge identification and solution, and may operate in a secondary process manner often drawing from experience and skills.

Conversely, the right hemisphere is necessary for the mental agility and intuitive associations that are also a requirement in the creative process and may operate in a primary processing manner (Galin, 1974; Hoppe, 1977). In other words, whereas much of our schooling and socialization probably prepared us for predominantly left-hemisphere activities and thought processes, being creative requires *spherical* thinking, and the coordinated use of both left and right halves of the brain.

Spherical thinking

'You have to live spherically in many directions - never lose your childish enthusiasm and things will come your way.'

Federico Fellini

Using both halves of the brain together does, of course, require that they are able to communicate with each other, which they do through the wide, flat bundle of axons beneath the brain's cortex called the corpus callosum. Considering the staggering capacity of the human brain in certain areas (pattern recognition, for example) it is quite surprising that something as apparently important as communication between the two hemispheres should occur through a communication channel as limited as the corpus callosum. It seems to be *dial-up* speed where you'd expect *broadband*!

In general, as primates developed so did the size of their brains. Along with that, the diameter of the axons, across which communication occurs, also increased. This maintained the speed of communication between the two cerebral hemispheres, particularly between motor and sensory areas, despite the increase in overall size. Strangely, this scaling, or increase in size of the corpus callosum with brain size, did not continue between the chimpanzee and the human. This means that the delay time between human hemispheres is twice what it is in the macaque monkey!

Anything we can do, then, to increase communication efficiency through the corpus callosum can only improve our ability to think creatively. There are two possibilities that have been documented. First, the corpus callosum in those who have been taught to play a musical instrument at a young age has been found to be larger than those who were not (Levitin, 2006). That may be because of the 'whole brain' nature of playing music. Interesting though that may be it doesn't help you much if you were not taught music at a young age. There is, however, a way in which we can influence, not corpus callosum size, but efficiency. It seems that if you do something that is physically repetitive but not psychologically demanding (going for a walk, for example), the 'data rate' across the corpus callosum increases significantly. Ever had an Ah ha! moment when you are out for a stroll? That may be why. The other activity that seems to be conducive to idea generation and problem solving, possibly partly for the same reason, is meditation. Meditating with a mantra could facilitate the same kind of communication improvement mentioned above. However, thinking a mantra is not actually a physical task, so this is just conjecture.

The third physical factor that has been found to be related to creativity is cortical activity. Broadly, this is how active our brains are at any moment, and it is easily measured by EEG: The higher an EEG frequency (and the lower its amplitude), the higher our level of cortical activity. When we are sleeping our cortical activity is low and when we are tense or anxious it is high. Martindale (1999) draws a parallel between this and primary /secondary processing. In other words, when we are sleeping, dozing or day dreaming he suggests we may be subject to low cortical activity and prone to primary processing. When we are 'hyped up' we are subject to high cortical activity and secondary processing. Although the relationship between creativity and cortical activity is not a linear one and is difficult to establish directly, it does seem that low levels of cortical activity are more conducive to creative thought than high levels. This is another reason why meditation, and its tendency to slow down our activity levels, might be conducive to idea generation and creativity.

Both Osgood (1960) and Meisels (1967) showed that increased levels of cortical activity are associated with more stereotyped writing (suggesting reduced creativity). Factors such as stress (Coren & Schulman, 1971; Horton, Marlow, & Crowne, 1963) and even the mere presence of others (Zajonc, 1965) increase cortical activity, and are also likely to have a negative influence on creativity. In terms of tackling problems, it seems that complex tasks are better performed at relatively low levels of cortical activity (possibly because they require more of the primary processing associated with intuition). Simple tasks, however, are better performed at relatively high levels of cortical activity, possibly because they may be more tolerant of a higher degree of focus and are less dependent on creative thought.

As you can see there are many factors that researchers have identified as having the potential to influence individual-level creativity. An important point which bears repeating is that while I do not believe we are all equally creative, I am not alone in believing that we are all born with a considerable capacity to be creative, and this gets socialized out of us. From an organizational perspective, then, we must create an environment where people can be confident in their right to individual expression and do not feel they have to perpetually hide within the bounds of a team. We want them to have the confidence to try out their ideas or opinions even if they fail to garner the support of others. The negative consequences of individuals *not* being able to feel confident in this way may have much more dramatic consequences than creative performance, as the Challenger space shuttle disaster attests[7]. We also want people to be comfortable and relaxed and to have some degree of autonomy. We don't want them to feel that they have evaluators breathing down their necks the whole time.

---

[7] The Challenger disaster has often been cited as resulting (among other causes) from Groupthink. **Groupthink** occurs when members of a decision making group trying to minimize conflict and reaching consensus without fully evaluating or vocalizing their ideas. Individual creativity, uniqueness, and independent thinking are lost in the pursuit of group agreement. There are several possible motives for Groupthink, including the desire to avoid embarrassment or being seen as foolish, or a desire to avoid angering other members of the group (including superiors). Individual doubts can be set aside (as in the case of discussions about the O rings in the Challenger), for fear of upsetting the group's balance.

The possible influences of stress

The previous paragraph illustrates that stress can have a negative influence on creativity – possibly because of the increase in cortical activity associated with it. However, there is some evidence that this is not always the case. Baer (1998) found a positive relationship; Amabile, Goldfarb, and Brackfield (1990) found a negative one, and Landon and Suedfeld (1972) found a curvilinear relationship between stress and creativity (i.e. with part of the relationship being linear and the lower and upper portions being non-linear). In a meta-analysis Byron, Khazanchi and Nazarian (2010) found a '… curvilinear relationship between evaluative stress and creativity such that low evaluative contexts *increased* creative performance over control conditions, whereas highly evaluative contexts *decreased* creative performance.' They also found that a sense of not being in control decreased creative performance. They conclude that '… results suggest that stressors' effects on creativity are more complex than previously assumed.'

In reviewing studies of healthcare workers, West and Sacramento (2006) found high (but not excessive) work demands to be associated with individual innovation (Bunce & West, 1995; West, 1989). They go on to conclude, however, that external demands inhibit creativity that occurs in the early stages of innovation (i.e. during ideation) but facilitate the implementation stages (which are probably less dependent on creative processes). These studies seem to suggest that external motivation can impact innovation in a positive way but not at the most creative stage.

In one of my own experiments (Walton, 2006), one group of participants, in the 'stressed' condition, read that they worked for a music promotion company whose survival depends on the success of their next musical production. Participants were then asked to think of as many creative ideas as possible to promote this concert. Creativity in this group was greater than the control group (whose organization was not fighting for its survival). However, in another experiment when the creativity task could not possibly be construed as helping the ailing organization (participants had to think of as many uses as possible for a common object, in this case a brick), participants' creativity was reduced by the stress of the organizational survival cue (in line with Byron, Khazanchi and Nazarian's findings regarding 'uncontrollability' decreasing creativity). In other words, 'fiddling while Rome burns' and doing a task perceived as irrelevant to mitigating the stress, reduces people's motivation to be creative. But being, to some extent at least, in control of one's destiny by being creative in a useful way seems to have the potential for a positive effect.

The message here is clear: If our creative organization is fighting for its survival (or even just to meet a deadline), employees need to feel that their creative problem solving efforts are contributing to the problem solution. Otherwise creativity levels seem to be reduced by stress and failure maybe a self-fulfilling prophecy!

Chapter 6 – Leading for Creativity

'Management is doing things right,
leadership is doing the right things.'

Peter Drucker

The unfortunate thing about chapters and books on leadership style is that for every leadership model you read about, the next successful leader you meet in real life seems to have many characteristics that are contrary to the model! An important first point, which is rather obvious, but needs to be stated nonetheless, is that management and leadership are not the same. The American political leader, educator, orator and author, Booker T. Washington said: "There are two ways of exerting one's strength: One is pushing down, the other is pulling up." In other words, the leader is sometimes distinguished from the manager by being the one that pulls up rather than pushes down. Another way of saying this is: Leaders have followers, managers have sub-ordinates.

A6.1 In the context of the GAM, what characteristics do you think a leader should have if stimulation of creativity is the goal.

Despite wide differences in the styles of leaders, there are several characteristics that successful leaders tend to share. First, they often seem to make one of their priorities keeping an eye on the future. Whatever else is going on they make sure they have a little time and energy to see all the possibilities regarding where the organization could be heading. Second, they tend to initiate systems, programs and structure (including goals). Third, they tend to be realistic in their demands of people and considerate in what they ask of them and how they ask it. They recognize people's individuality and their ability to contribute, and are tolerant of their failures. Forth, they are able to think and communicate clearly and unambiguously.

In the context of creating the innovative organization of the new era, the difference between leading and managing is particularly important. The notion of people *following* a leader suggests intrinsic motivation. In other words they accept the guidance of another because it makes sense and they respect the leader and *want to* follow his or her decisions. The idea of employees being *pushed* to do something by a manager, however, suggests something quite opposite. It is the voluntary (and intrinsic) desire to do one's job in a creative way that we are seeking; the top down approach is not conducive to creative thought or action.

The attributes characterizing good leadership mentioned above are important in generating a creative environment. Creative employees need their space and they need to be seen to be individuals, but they will also be at their most creative when they don't feel they have to be continually looking over their shoulders and worrying about the stability and future of the organization. (This would be associated with high cortical activity and could potentially undermine creative performance). Our creative organization, then, needs strong guidance, including clear, realistic goals which everyone feels they 'own'. Providing the 'space' for the expression of creativity and individuality does not equate to freewheeling or drifting. It is exciting to work within an organization lead by a futuristic thinker where employees feel that the leader is one step ahead of the competition. Even employees in organizations that are 'horizontally managed' (i.e. with a 'flat DMS' where management decisions are shared by many employees) need to feel that there is a strong leader at the helm.

Even though people like some degree of stability, to be creative they also need change. A charismatic leader who mixes things up by introducing new ideas and processes from time to time does a lot to prevent everyday activities becoming humdrum. That is good for innovation.

Hersey-Blanchard Situational Leadership

This is not a book about leadership theory specifically so I am not going to discuss all the different theories that have been propounded in the history of management. But I will mention a couple of established leadership models that have been reviewed at some length.

Back in the 1970s Hersey and Blanchard characterized styles of leadership in terms of the amount of Task Behavior and Relationship Behavior that a leader provides to his or her followers (Hersey & Blanchard, 1972). These leadership styles are characterized into four behavior types:

1. **Telling** - communication is one-way. The leader defines the roles of the individual or group and provides the what, how, when, and where to do the task.
2. **Selling** – the leader uses two-way communication and provides the support that will allow individuals or groups to buy into the process. The leader still provides direction.

3. **Participating** - decision making is now shared regarding aspects of how the task is accomplished. The leader provides less direct task related instruction.
4. **Delegating** - the leader is still involved in decisions. However, the direct responsibility for carrying out tasks is with the individual or group. The leader stays involved to monitor progress.

> **A6.2 Think about three or four organizations that you know something about and try and characterize their leadership styles in terms of Hersey and Blanchard's categories. Then try and rank the organizations in terms of how innovative you perceive them to be. Are the two related?**

Hersey and Blanchard did not consider any one of these styles to be optimal for all leaders to use in all situations. However, in the context of the twenty first century and our interest in creating an innovative organizational environment we might view this differently. While there may be a time and place for all four leadership styles, the first two may not do much to foster innovativeness. Our creative leader is likely to focus on using these in reverse order, delegating wherever possible.

Transformational and transactional leadership

Leadership can be viewed as a social process situated within a group context with a leader influencing the behavior of followers such that organizational goals are met. As a catalyst of desired behaviors the leader's role ranges from visionary, inspirational and motivational, on the one hand, to the design of an appropriate organizational context on the other. Bernard Bass and Bruce Avolio (1993) referred to these as transformational and transactional leadership styles. They suggested that "…transactional leaders work within their organizational cultures following existing rules, procedures, and norms; transformational leaders change their culture by first understanding it and then realigning the organization's culture with a new vision and a revision of its shared assumptions, values, and norms" (Bass, 1985).

Transformational leadership is said to be characterized by four elements: *idealized influence,* whereby trust and confidence is elicited through charismatic behavior; *intellectual stimulation,* which encourages others to question assumptions and adopt new approaches; *inspirational motivation,* using enthusiasm to communicate ideas and goals; and, *individualized consideration,* or treating everyone as an individual, mentoring them and considering their needs.

In an organization headed by a transactional leader the focus is on individuals having a task clearly explained to them along with the reward for its completion or corrective action for failure. In other words (and somewhat oversimplified) it is management by reward/punishment. There is no shortage of leaders who have achieved ambitious and challenging goals through transactional leadership. A recent example is European Business Leader of the Year for 2008, Sergio Marchionne, who turned automaker Fiat around with a new organizational structure and a new, clear set of goals for all to follow.

At first glance transformational leadership may seem the more likely contender for the leadership style of our innovative organization. It is in many ways more dynamic and more conducive to constant re-evaluation and change. On the other hand, following Marchionne's powerful demonstration that there can still be life in a European auto manufacturer, Fiat is now an innovative business under transactional leadership!

The point here is that there is a place for both leadership styles. In some ways they are more complementary than they are contradictory. Transactional leadership is more aligned in many ways with traditional management objectives and techniques and this can be a powerful tool alongside someone with a less conventional pattern of leadership behaviors. Some employees (particularly those with a low tolerance for ambiguity) find the erratic tendencies of Apple's Steve Jobs' style of leadership difficult to work with. On the other hand it can be very conducive to a creative environment where the *we have never done it that way,* or the *it isn't part of the plan* school have little place.

The well-led organization

Whatever the leadership style, there are several characteristics shared by 'well-led' innovative organizations and it is, perhaps, more important to focus on these than it is to debate which leadership or management route should be used to achieve them. In practice, prospective leaders do not stand in front of the mirror before they launch their organizations trying out different 'hats' to see which they prefer. Certain individual characteristics are conducive to certain leadership styles and people will only achieve leadership success if they are comfortable within the context of their leadership style (which is not to say that experience and training cannot help managers make adjustments to their leadership techniques in order to help them be more effective).

Organizational innovation is a positively reinforced phenomenon. In other words, organizations that have generated a creative product find it easier to do so again. In part this is because the individuals within the organization (including management) now have every reason to be confident in the value of innovation. There is, if you like, visible evidence of the power of creativity and its value to the group and the individuals within it. To some considerable degree the act of being successfully creative can change the institutional norm to one that is supportive of creativity *de facto*. The other way in which having been innovative helps an organization be innovative again, is that the chain of events that leads to the final product, process or change requires core skills, and these skills get honed with practice. These skills will vary depending on the type of organization and the type of innovations or changes being introduced. These changes are often subtle, and they are often a mix of individual processes and team work. As with the use of any other skill, the first innovation may be the most difficult.

The other way in which innovation is a positively reinforcing phenomenon is that there is a positive link (in both directions) between being creative, and mood. In other words doing something creative tends to have a positive impact on one's mood, and people of positive mood seem also to be more creative (Wright & Staw, 1999; Wright & Walton, 2003).

A6.3 Can you think of any physiological reason why a good mood might be conducive to creative?

One possible reason for the correlation between positive affect and creativity is described by a phenomenon called mood congruence. We tend to best remember events that were experienced and committed to memory in our current mood (Clark & Teasdale, 1985). So when we are happy we will tend to recall happy times more easily than sad events, and vice versa. Most psychologically healthy people have more happy memories than sad ones, so when we are trying to come up with new ideas and be creative, happy people will tend to have more readily recallable experiences to draw on than sad people.

A further reason why positive affect and creativity are positively related could be cortical activity. Nervousness and stress tend to increase cortical activity and decrease creative abilities, whereas a relaxed atmosphere, i.e. one conducive to positive mood, will be associated with lower levels of cortical activity and higher levels of creativity.

If for no other reason than generating an atmosphere conducive to creativity, a leadership style and organizational structure that encourages employees and associates to be positive, happy and upbeat is an important attribute.

Leadership of the start-up

When small entrepreneurial start-up businesses, built around an invention or innovative idea, grow into bigger businesses they often seem to lose their innovativeness. Although this is most obvious in commercial enterprises it can be equally true of social entrepreneurial groups. The founder was often crucial to the original idea and subsequently becomes buried in the day-to-day activities of running the organization, losing the motivation or resources to innovate. From a GAM perspective this might be because the founder no longer has the facility to 'leave the group' in order to create; he or she is expected to be fully present at all times (or that is how the situation may be perceived anyway).

Also the original idea or invention may have been generated in an atmosphere of 'play' with little in the way of pressure regarding success, failure or timeframe; in other words, the invention emerged from ideas upon which nothing really depended. At that point no one's livelihood hung in the balance. Down the road when the start-up has developed into the not-quite-so-small organization, things feel very different. Now the leader may have given up his/her day job to run the business fulltime and there are employees that rely on the solvency of the company for their wellbeing. This is a very different setting from which to invest funds and other resources in developing new products or processes, and a very different environment in which to try to generate new ideas.

A third reason for the frequent decline in inventiveness in emerging small and medium enterprises (SMEs) may be that start-up entrepreneurs tend to set their sights rather low. One large-scale study found that only 10% of all start-up entrepreneurs expected to create 20 or more jobs within 5 years (Autio, 2007). Low ambitions could be associated with low levels of motivation to innovate. The argument could run: "How can we justify investing in new product/services when we have so far to go to fully exploit what we have?" Whatever the reasons for the reduced levels of innovation, evolving from the start-up stage to a level where management tasks become more challenging requires a new skill set (Zahra, Filatotchev, & Wright, 2009); one that may be quite different from those needed initially.

Leading for diversity

I will discuss the stages involved in the innovative process in greater detail later; but let us say that we are trying to solve a particular problem, meet a challenge, or generate a new product or process. An important step is to 'lay out' (figuratively or literally) all the ideas that we can lay our hands on regarding how we might address the particular challenge. At a later stage these ideas will be analyzed and filtered, but for now the goal is to produce as many unique ideas as possible, however zany. This process is generally done by a group of people (via brainstorming, for instance); the idea being more people will generate more ideas. To some extent this is true, although, as you might expect, the law of diminishing returns tends to apply as people generate duplicate ideas with increasing frequency as membership in the group increases.

A6.4 Focusing on an organization that you are part of or are familiar with, take a careful look at the employees or associates that you know. Is there a high degree of diversity regarding social, ethnic and religious backgrounds? Is there a similar number of women and men working there? Are they predominantly old, young or a mixture? Do you think it is quite a creative organization?

This is an important process and I will return to it in the next chapter. For now, though, I will focus on the composition of the group. Individuals are generally chosen for inclusion in teams or groups because of their compatibility with other group members. It feels comfortable to be working alongside people who are likeminded. The problem is that likeminded people tend not to produce the same diversity of ideas as people who do not share many personality characteristics or experiences with other group members. Also, the process of innovation does not end with idea generation. Ideas have to be put into some kind of order, a plan generated and then the road map followed to its conclusion, when the new product or process emerges. It should come as no surprise that we are not all equally good at each stage of the innovation process. Idea generators may not be the best people to create and follow a methodical plan. Individual characteristics, then, predispose different people to different stages in the innovative process (Basadur & Head, 2001; Basadur & Gelade, 2002). This is yet another reason why diversity is important in the innovative team.

Diversity has other potential advantages as well as in the area of innovation. In today's global community businesses are increasingly selling their products across ethnic and other boundaries, both through exporting and domestically. High diversity helps overcome tendencies towards a 'not-invented-here' mentality, and it also helps generate feedback during product development regarding suitability for different geographically and socially defined markets.

During the development stage of a microphone that I invented and brought to market back in the 1980s, a born-again Christian employee of mine took me aside one day and said that one of the markets we had in mind might well alienate us if we only manufactured our mic in black (we were planning on marketing our products for use on acoustic pianos, and churches had been identified as significant potential customers). It had not occurred to me that our black microphone might be associated with anything satanic, but we added the question to others that were asked of a focus group and my employee was found to be correct. Our mic was eventually manufactured in brown and churches became one of our largest purchasers!

As well as seeking diversity for creativity reasons, one of the things we are trying to achieve in our innovative organization is the matching of tasks with individual personality traits appropriate to them. In other words we are looking for a best fit between people's skills, desires and individual traits, and their responsibilities. As an example, in my manufacturing company (that made the brown microphones) I was a rather 'Steve Jobsian' kind of leader. It was common for me to return from a trip and unfold ideas for new products or for changes in existing products or processes. I was impatient and uncomfortable waiting for organizational growth to occur at its natural pace (if there is such a thing). This tendency to erraticism is something I became acutely aware of (indeed, it was difficult to miss!), so I tried to surround myself with one or two managers who were what I call 'pipe and slippers' people. This role happened to be filled by men, although it need not have been.

> **A6.5 Thinking again about the organization that you focused on in A6.4 ask yourself: 'Do you think it is quite a creative organization?'**
>
> Are there decisions that are made within the organization that could or do benefit from its diversity?

'Pipe and slippers' people are definitely 'local' rather than 'global'. They tend to resist change, they are reliable and they are 'home bodies'. They prefer to be beside the fire wearing slippers, smoking a pipe (smoking was less stigmatized in those days!) with a dog at their feet, than going exploring. I always knew the factory doors would be unlocked at precisely 8.00 a.m. every morning whether I was there or not. These managers would also sigh deeply on hearing my new ideas unfold, knowing the status quo that they clung on to with fervor was about to be threatened. Some of their objections to my ideas were transparent attempts to resist change, but some of them were valid reflections of a different viewpoint; a viewpoint that cast doubts that in my enthusiasm and optimism I had missed or minimized. It was a useful and valuable foil that contributed a great deal to the development of a growth strategy that embraced change - but not at any price.

As well as to comply with antidiscrimination laws, there are many positive reasons, then, to embrace diversity among the managers and employees in our innovative organization: diversity of ethnicity, gender, personality type, demography, religion, ... diversity along more dimensions the better! Just as there are many varied day to day roles that different people are best suited to, so there are many roles in the innovation process that different types of people perform best. There is evidence that certain psychological traits seem to relate to idea generation, and there are certainly others that are invaluable when taking a creative idea to its innovative conclusion.

Diversity does, however, present new management challenges at individual, team and organizational levels. For instance, we have to be more careful when communicating with those who are different from us, in order to be effective and unambiguous. You are more likely to be misunderstood or misinterpreted in a diverse environment. Your motives will sometimes be questioned in ways you would never have anticipated, and there will be

---

Guidance from the East

The ancient Indian 'science of life' *ayurveda* defines different body and personality types. Depak Chopra describes this medical philosophy along with the ayurvedic body types, or *doshas*, and how they are influenced, in many of his books, including *Perfect Health* and *Quantum Healing*. Briefly, there are three doshas each of which has certain physiological and psychological traits associated with it. One's health, according to ayurveda, depends on the balance of the doshas. Erraticism of the type I have described is a typical *vata* trait, and the 'pipe and slippers' quality epitomizes *kapha*. There is a third type, *pitta*, which is often noticeable through a sharp wit and fiery temper. Just as individuals need to balance the doshas to be healthy, perhaps organizations should also?

new demands made of you. The resulting organizational environment, however, is rich in experience, and this is what we need as the foundation of the creative company.

A6.6 What do you think the main challenges might be managing a highly diverse team rather than a homogenous one?

The key to managing a diverse team is flexibility, understanding and authenticity. Decide what core factors in the organization are immutable and what are not. Is it vital for everyone to arrive and leave at the same time? How flexible can we be without making it impossible to get everyone together? Is there room in the organizational process for people to spend time working from home? Can we organize projects to be team rather than individual responsibilities and then allow teams to establish their own rules of functioning?

These are the kinds of questions that need addressing when we are structuring our innovative team in order to leave plenty of room for autonomy, individuality and diversity. Remember, we are trying to create an environment that nurtures and positively supports creativity and innovation, *and*, we want our environment to be attractive to creative people we may wish to hire in the future. For some businesses the kind of change I am describing is a dramatic upheaval, but the price for *not* doing it may be extinction!

Other leadership traits

There are several traits that I and others have observed in successful and creative leaders. This is not a complete list since factors discussed elsewhere such as dedication and persistence are also crucial to success. Also, the characteristics listed below when taken individually may not amount to much, but taken as a whole they provide a potent complement to the other attributes discussed.

• **Listening & learning.** Part of what innovation and good leadership is about is data collection - from all sources. We are wasting our time creating new processes or products if they are not appropriate or what people want. We can only discover that by listening. That is a crucial part of the first step in the innovation cycle.

Trade shows are expensive to attend and often produce results that are difficult to quantify. If they are being honest, most entrepreneurs or managers find it difficult to justify the time and money involved in taking booth space based on immediate sales alone. One of my mentors in the early days of my entrepreneurship told me that the most important activity at a trade show was listening! Decades later I am still convinced he was right. Effective and innovative leaders know when and to whom to listen.

- **Men & women of action.** Without exception the successful leaders I have worked with have been *doers*. They have meetings, make decisions, establish goals and get on with it ... immediately! This has several observable effects. First, it sets the example to everyone in the business that goals, decisions and plans are not for show, they are there to be implemented; this is not 'busy work'. If the boss is thrusting forward everyone else had better do the same – or get left behind. Second, it helps provide an icon for the whole organization. Everyone wants to work for someone they respect, and that others respect also. Being a man or woman of action is part of that. Finally, it gets the job done! The cost of implementing a plan is strongly related to the time taken to do it. The longer the clock ticks the more overhead costs accrue before the end result emerges. In commercial organizations in increasingly competitive markets launching products or implementing processes sooner rather than later can establish technologies as 'cutting edge', and helps position the business as market leader.

- **Compassion.** As mentioned before, employees have a different perspective regarding choosing their employers now than they did in the past. They want to be proud of their employer and they want to be treated in a human way, with compassion. They also want flexibility and facilities that enable them to put their families first. IBM is typical of many large companies: around 60% of its employee population is dual income, 30% are women, and 30% need to provide some kind of care for an elderly relative. IBM has an edge in attracting and retaining high-quality staff through benefits such as flexible work schedules, temporary part-time work arrangements, provision of child care, and work-at-home possibilities. They see these kinds of work-life programs and benefits as powerful motivators

---

Dealing with tragedy: Starbucks

Starbucks is known for its exceptional treatment of employees, offering medical insurance, for instance, even to part-time workers. In 1997 tragedy struck when three employees were killed in an attempted robbery of one of its Washington D.C. outlets. Starbuck's CEO, Howard Schultz, flew to D.C. and spent the week with employees, their families, and the families of the deceased. Schultz's personal compassion and compassionate leadership did a great deal to mitigate the tragedy.

---

that stimulate productivity and employee loyalty and promote the appropriate image to attract and retain top personnel. But, compassion is not just about benefits and flexible work schedules; it is about leaders genuinely caring for employees *as people,* as Howard Schultz did in dealing with Starbucks' tragedy. At first glance this may not seem to have much to do with creativity, but it does. An atmosphere of compassion and understanding generates the notion that 'it is OK to fail' because management will understand. Also, employees tend to be given individual attention in a compassionate environment, which is conducive to an individualistic norm.

Finally you tend not to feel you have to be 'looking over your shoulder' in a compassionate organization. No one is going to send you a memo telling you to clear your desk and be out in an hour – you've been downsized! Might you get dismissed in a compassionate environment? Of course. But it is likely to happen in a way that softens the blow, with a longer-than-necessary notice period or with some suggestions and help regarding other work possibilities. This kind of environment is conducive to a relaxed atmosphere which, as noted earlier, encourages creativity for both psychological and physiological reasons. Compassion costs little and creates powerful motivators for creativity: respect and loyalty.

- **Authenticity**. The news is replete with corporate heads proclaiming one thing and doing another: mourning the necessity of layoffs while taking record-breaking bonuses; proclaiming the necessity of

> *Definition:* Kernis and Goldman (2005) defined authenticity as the "unobstructed operation of one's true or core self in one's daily enterprise" (p. 32).

cutbacks while using the corporate jet for family fun. As knowledge of these practices erodes employee confidence, so authenticity goes a long way to generating a loyal and successful organization. Behind the name tag 'Jim' is Costco head Jim Sinegal. Costco attracts the most affluent customers in discount retailing - with an average income of $74,000. Sales in 2009 totaled more than $52 billion from 462 stores in 37 states and 8 countries, yet Jim pays himself only $350,000 a year (based on about 12 times the salary of the typical worker on the floor). This authenticity along with better-than-average benefits and wages (around 40% higher than WalMart's Sams Club) help explain why Costco has one of the lowest rates of employee turnover in retailing (about 1/5 of WalMart's).

In humanistic and phenomenological models of the human psyche well-being and authenticity are intimately linked, with authenticity meaning 'being true to oneself'. This perspective emphasizes self-expression, self-awareness, and self-determination as important attributes (Deci & Ryan, 1985; Rogers, 1961). Also, authenticity has been associated with clarity regarding one's self-concept, mindfulness and vitality, ability to implement adaptive coping strategies, and the tendency to react less defensively than those with low authenticity (Kernis & Goldman, 2006). As with creativity, however, not all contexts promote authenticity equally (Sheldon, Ryan, Rawsthorne, & Ilardi, 1997). For example, it may be difficult to be fully authentic if your lifestyle preferences or religious beliefs are unusual, and you work in a highly conservative organization. The organization's norms may tolerate only a narrow range of behaviors.

Other links between authenticity and creativity may not be immediately obvious, but the innovative environment we are trying to create is not composed of a few obvious factors, it comprises many subtle ones which, taken in isolation, may not seem that important. When these are added together, however, wonderful things can happen. Authenticity helps people feel safe. It is the opposite of the 'hidden agenda' that tends to make employees feel on edge and suspicious of management motives. When people feel safe they tend to be happier, more stress free and more creative (Claxton, 1997; Claxton, 1998; Wright & Walton, 2003).

- **Simplicity.** One of the traits that I have observed in competent and innovative leaders is a respect for simplicity. Even when a problem or challenge is complex their methodologies suggest a belief that inside every complex

> Inside every complex problem are lots of simple problems trying to get out

problem are lots of simple problems trying to get out! Consider the process of inventing a new product or process; when the challenge requires a complex solution it is very difficult to treat it in a unique way. We tend to gravitate towards thinking schematically, stringing existing solutions together. However, when a problem can be viewed as straightforward or simple then it is much easier for us to generate creative, non-schematic solutions. Part of Costco's genius is its simplicity. A typical Wal-Mart stocks more than 100,000 items, Costco stocks only 4,000 (that is not to suggest that WalMart is not also a highly successful organization, it is). Costco doesn't have a P.R. department and it doesn't spend a dime on advertising. That is simplicity!

PART 2 – Techniques and Practices in Innovative Organizations

In this section of the book I look at the tools available to us regarding how to put creativity to work in our organization of the new era. In doing so I talk about groups and teams as well as individuals, and I discuss many situational factors that influence us both in and outside our places of work. For instance, there are powerful forces from the social web surrounding us, in the form of group norms, i.e. the offer of support or the threat of admonishment for approved of or unapproved of activities. These influence our motivation to be creative. In other words, society and our ingroups form the milieu within which creativity either flourishes or wilts.

Ultimately, however influential the social forces, the act of generating unique ideas is an individual activity, although the process of going from idea to innovation may well require others. It is important to know when group interaction and cooperation is appropriate and when it is individual thought that will be most productive. Remember that in the course of creative idea generation, the individual must depart, to some extent, from the comfort of his or her group, do the ideation, then rejoin the group. As with a departure and subsequent return from any journey, the relationship with the group is never quite the same. To accommodate this, the group needs to have some tolerance and flexibility in its attitudes towards dynamic qualities in its members.

In some creative endeavors the departure from the group may be literal and extensive in time. Many writers, poets and painters throughout history have traveled to remote corners of the world, sometimes for months or years, to catalyze their creativity. In an organizational context the departure may be more figurative than literal and the time away from the group may be brief, but the process of going through this 'departure-contemplation-return' cycle is an important one, that our 'organization of the new era' must accommodate within its leadership and organizational structure and norms.

Chapter 7 – Brainstorming

'The good ideas are all hammered out in agony by individuals,
not spewed out by groups'

Charles Brower

Brainstorming is an important tool for the innovative organization and is the idea generation stage or stages in the creative problem solving (CPS) process (which I discuss in some detail in the next chapter). However, there is no evidence that brainstorming in any way parallels what happens when people compose a piece of music or spontaneously invent a new product or process. So brainstorming is no substitute for creating an environment within which innovation and creativity can burgeon spontaneously. It was simply designed as an idea generation tool.

In some CPS tasks brainstorming is used to identify what the challenge or problem really is. For instance, a business might want to examine ways to become more profitable. Rather than jumping to the conclusion that increasing sales should be the main focus of effort, brainstorming may reveal other options that are also worth considering, which may end up being more immediate or requiring less investment.

Once this initial challenge is identified, the more traditional role of brainstorming can begin; i.e. generating 'how to' ideas regarding addressing the challenge. Frequently brainstormers have already had the challenge identified for them (by upper management or the Board, for instance) so they start at this second stage. Either way, a successful brainstorming session requires detailed planning, and its success depends on diligence implementation.

There are several stages in planning a brainstorming session, including:

- Deciding who will be part of the brainstorming team
- Choosing a facilitator and venue
- Establishing the rules

Building the team

Choosing the right individuals to participate in a brainstorming session is crucial to the success of the process. The brainstorming team may meet once or twice to establish how to identify and meet a specific challenge or, less commonly, it may be ongoing. Teams that meet regularly and often are rare but it can be a good idea when either the purpose of the organization is to generate creative ideas (i.e., an advertising company), or when a project is complex and lengthy (designing the space shuttle, for instance). In the latter case the team often acts in a regulatory capacity also, monitoring progress as well as generating new ideas regarding overcoming ongoing hurdles. Either way, when a team such as this (or a focus group) meets on an ongoing basis, it is a good idea to rotate group membership. In a team of five or six people, change two of them after, say, three meetings. It is the responsibility of those that remain in the group to bring the new members up to speed (helped by notes and summaries from previous meetings). The result can be a fresh start, just when it is needed, with new ideas and new enthusiasm.

One challenge when setting up a brainstorming group is that of finding a balance between diversity and comfort. Highly diverse groups can be difficult to facilitate and communication can be a challenge because of sparse areas of common ground. However, they can also be very exhilarating and a rich source of unique ideas. The comfortable solution, where team members are from similar backgrounds and experiences, and know each other well, is decidedly less effective at idea generation.

Perhaps because of confidentiality issues, brainstorming teams are often 'in-house' and comprised solely of employees. Partly for the reasons outlined in the previous paragraph, this is also likely to limit the scope of ideas generated. We all know that an outsider's view of our group or organization is different, sometimes *very* different, from our own. For that reason it is a good idea to find an external person or people to participate in the brainstorming, even if it is just the facilitator. The challenge then becomes how much information they are given before the brainstorming session. My suggestion is none or very little. This forces someone in the group to present a focused and thorough summary of the relevant background and why the brainstorming session is being conducted. Having an external presence in the group ensures that this summary contains plenty of basic detail. Without an external presence it might be (erroneously) assumed that everyone in the group already knows all this information, and shares a common understanding of the challenge at hand.

Choosing a facilitator

The facilitator introduces the session, and may present the background information. He or she is also the timekeeper and polices the process to make sure the rules are followed. The facilitator is crucial to the smooth running of the session and to the degree of participation and comfort of all participants. Without a competent facilitator so called brainstorming sessions can revert to a competitive opinion-peddling process, with those with greater power or particularly extravert personalities, 'winning'. Also, if the ideation process stagnates, the facilitator is responsible for kick-starting it. The role of the facilitator is an important one and a professional is often chosen since it really does require experience in how to stimulate every group member to generate novel ideas, and how to deal with different personality types simultaneously.

If, for budgetary or other reasons, it is decided not to use a professional brainstorming facilitator, then consider using someone from outside the group whose background or status within the organization is not known to group members. Have them introduce themselves in a very general way that does not imply status or suggest to group members that they might have any kind of hidden agenda. "Good morning, I am Andrew Webber from HR…" for instance, may leave group members feeling reticent about participating in case any observations about their personality or performance get into their employee records. "Good morning, I am Andrew Webber, I am in sales…" may be less threatening.

Choosing a venue

It is important that brainstorming participants are encouraged to think differently during the session. This is not, by definition, a natural process and everything we can do to promote it will be of benefit; for instance, by having participants dress casually. If participants can be persuaded to dress in a way that helps them express their personalities (rather than generic jeans) I find this can help them explore new ways of thinking.

By default most brainstorming sessions seem to take place in the organization's conference or board room. I think this is a bad idea. The challenge is to get everyone to think in ways that they are not used to and to cultivate new cognitive pathways, so any cues that you can use to achieve that will pay dividends. Familiar surroundings (particularly ones with formal associations) tend to generate familiar patterns of thinking and activity, and one of the things we are often trying to achieve is to get team members to take a fresh look at the organization. Taking people into a new environment helps break molds and stimulates the generation of new ideas. My local library used to have some very interesting painting and sculpture exhibitions from time to time, and they also had a comfortable meeting room. It was well suited to brainstorming sessions. The art exhibitions provided a creative and enjoyable change of pace and stimulated discussion outside of the brainstorming topic during our breaks.

> **A7.1 Can you recall when you had an Ah-ha! moment? What was the environment and what were you doing at the time?**

I mentioned earlier that the left and right hemispheres of the brain communicate better with each other when we are doing something mechanical that does not require much thought (like walking). One thing I try and do, then, is to organize brainstorming sessions to include spaces where people can stroll around and contemplate individually. So a garden or pleasant grassy area or something similar is an asset; ambling through an art gallery is a reasonable indoor alternative.

Obviously creature comforts need to be attended to when choosing a venue. People do not think in a divergent and creative way if they are cold, hot, thirsty, hungry or in pain through sitting on a hard chair for too long! A choice of seating is especially useful for individual thinking times for those who do not want to, or cannot, walk around. I have even seen bean bags brought into the brainstorming environment to serve this purpose.

Establishing the rules

Participants need to have a background to the problem or challenge. Those from outside the organization may need an outline of the business, products or purposes of the organization and the broad subject area of the brainstorming session.

1. The background and session purpose need to be clearly presented (preferably by the facilitator) in some detail at the beginning of the session.

2. Brainstorming is a time for creative thinking, not judgment. Judgmental or critical comments erode the creative process. They are inappropriate at this stage.

3. Brainstorming sessions should be loose, lighthearted and fun. Having fun is conducive to being creative. Humor is a great stimulator of

creativity, so don't suppress jokes; they can be used to catalyze people into generating ideas.

4. Everyone needs to participate. Human nature dictates that some people will be more vocal and forceful than others, but we need ideas from everyone in the group. Often ideas from more introverted participants will be quite different from those from extraverts, and it is important that we get those too.

5. Make sure you have plenty of pencils, paper, flip charts and markers of different colors, and Post-it notes (particularly the large ones). All ideas need to be written down and Post-it's are useful for this as they can be stuck together to group ideas.

6. Set guidelines regarding the minimum and maximum length of time the session should take. It is important for the facilitator to stick to this since brainstorming will only be a part of the overall CPS process. Setting goals regarding how many unique ideas needs to be generated is suggested by some facilitators, although I have never found this necessary. More often, we need to whittle the idea pool down to a manageable size.

The brainstorming session

As I discussed earlier, brainstorming, as a group activity, is antithetical to creativity. In other words the process tends to make group membership more salient than individuality, which is not conducive to creative idea generation. What we have to do, then, is to establish phases within the brainstorming session when individuals work on their own before they come together to share their ideas.

After introductions and the background to and purpose of the session, the facilitator should introduce the challenge, at the broadest possible level: Perhaps the brainstorming session came about because the board decided that the business needed to be more involved in the local community. Rather than talking about charitable donations or sponsorship, the facilitator might introduce the challenge simply as: "How can [our organization] best be more involved in the community?" The traditional solutions such as charitable giving, sponsoring youth groups etc. will emerge from the process but by presenting the challenge in a broad way other, perhaps more effective or practical, ideas may also emerge. Each participant should write this challenge at the top of a blank sheet of paper.

70

At this stage I have the group break out and individual participants are encouraged to go spend some time, perhaps fifteen minutes, by themselves generating and writing down their ideas regarding how to address the challenge. I encourage people to walk about outside or possibly in a different area of the facility. When everyone reconvenes the facilitator asks them to go around in turn and read their ideas to the group *from their list*. The act of writing and then reading their ideas helps prevent individuals from feeling intimidated by the group or by specific others. In other words it encourages them to share ideas that they might otherwise suppress in case they were thought stupid or inappropriate. I request a volunteer from the group to pool ideas on a flip chart. This type of brainstorming is often the first or second stage in CPS.

Once ideas are pooled they can be grouped together with other similar ideas. This process often helps people generate new, novel ideas that weren't on their original list, so I generally suggest that, once again as individuals, we take some time to generate new ideas. Often when team members come together again they are keen to expand on the ideas of others and then distill the idea pool down to a manageable number of ideas. At this point it is important not to dismiss any idea; all efforts are focused on being *con*structive.

The next stage depends on the purpose of the brainstorming session. It may be one stage in a structured CPS process (which will be discussed in more detail in the next chapter) or it may simply be to generate ideas for further development. An advertising agency, for instance, may want a wide spread of ideas regarding the promotion of a client's new product line. They might take the brainstorming ideas and 'visualize' them to see which direction the client wants to go in; so zany ideas might co-exist alongside more traditional ones.

Either way, at some stage, the ideas will be 'distilled', and some criteria used to weed out those considered impractical or undesirable for some reason or another. It is critical that the weeding out is conducted with as much integrity as the brainstorming itself, or the agnostic and non-judgmental atmosphere of a well-conducted brainstorming session is wasted. In particular, the distillation process needs to be free of any intra-organizational agenda. I strongly suggest that the non-organizational team members stay onboard for the distillation process to help monitor the objective nature of this important stage.

Stimulating idea generation

When we are using brainstorming to generate ideas there can be times when things seem to get 'stuck' and ideas simply aren't emerging. 'Stuckness' can be catching and happens more frequently in the traditional team ideation environment than the individual technique that I recommend. Nonetheless, the generation of ideas can dry up or we may feel that we have not yet tapped all possibilities for a particular challenge solution. There are a few techniques that can help.

Challenge inversion

Reversing a challenge or problem is a useful technique for stimulating ideas. It is easy to do, you simply ask the brainstorming group the opposite of the question that you *actually* want answers to and carry those ideas part way through the process.

For example, if you want to brainstorm ideas regarding how to improve customer relations, the question you actually ask would be 'How would I reduce the quality of our customer relations?' The kinds of answers that team members might generate include:
- Generate poor product documentation
- Use customer relations staff who have little training regarding the organization's products or services
- Ensure customer service staff are rude at all times
- Be slow to answer the customer help line
- Do not return customer calls promptly
- Do not follow through on commitments made to customers

The process can be amusing, which helps establish a lighthearted atmosphere that is conducive to the creative process, and the primary issues to be faced are sometimes more apparent when the challenge is reversed. Inverting the suggestions is generally a trivial process and forms a good basis for discussion.

Forced relationships

One of the challenges of brainstorming with team members from within the organization is to get those individuals to look afresh at the business (as if from the outside). *Forced relationships*[8] can help achieve this by asking team members to think of the organization's products or services in terms of a different industry. The facilitator might ask the question: "If this organization were a manufacturer of white goods which one would it be?" It is sometimes easier to see the branding and structure of other companies than it is our own and this helps us take a fresh look at our organization. You don't have to choose another type of organization for this exercise; the alternate image can be a person (i.e. a politician or an entertainer) or even a fish, insect or bird – anything that has common characteristics that are easily recognizable.

Forced analogy

The *Forced analogy* technique has similar goals to the *forced relationships* approach, but here we are using an analog for the problem or challenge being faced. The facilitator might ask the question: "How is the problem we are here to discuss similar to ..." The analogy inserted depends, of course, on the original problem. For instance, if an organization is trying to design a new type of scuba diving fin, the facilitator's question might be: "How is the problem we are here to discuss similar to designing footwear for walking on the moon?" This approach might show up issues such as: not wanting to disturb the ground to avoid generating a dust storm; or, how to keep a foot covering attached to the feet in a weightless environment; or, how to make walking easier in a cumbersome shoe or boot.

This technique is not an alternative to brainstorming, but it can provide a lighthearted and useful way for team members to start communicating with each other before generating ideas quickly and fluidly.

Whether it is a formal brainstorming session, a discussion, or just 'bouncing ideas around' our innovative organization needs to be continually on the lookout for creative ideas regarding every aspect of the business. Remember that creative ideas are not just a product of brainstorming sessions, they are the product of dissuading people from thinking in schemas, shifting them sideways into 'spaces' that they are not used to being in, and 'ringing the changes'. As long as you do not create fear and anxiety, taking people out of their comfort zone is an important part of generating creative ideas. If you have ever been on a "ropes

---

[8] Attributed to Charles Whiting

course[9]" you know that some people react very positively to being challenged when out of their comfort zone and others resist and resent it. In terms of creative idea generation it is important that we are upbeat and positive, so our organization will give people the opportunity to bring individuality into their work and their work environment without making that an overt requirement.

---

[9] A ropes course is a team building and personal development activity comprising activities at ground level and up in the trees. It is designed to take people out of their comfort zones before helping them confront their personal fears and phobias.

Chapter 8 – Creative Problem Solving (CPS)

'Imagination is more important than knowledge. For while knowledge defines all we currently know and understand, imagination points to all we might yet discover and create.'

Albert Einstein

First, I don't particularly like the phrase *creative problem solving*. The word *problem* has negative connotations that get us off to anything other than a light hearted, fun-loving start. Also, we are not always dealing with problems in the traditional sense. Sometimes we are looking to do things differently or expand some aspect of the organization's activities in some way. 'How do we involve ourselves more with the local community?' for instance, is a legitimate challenge for the CPS process, but it is hardly a *problem* in the usual meaning of the word. However, *creative problem solving* was coined a long time ago, by the originators of this kind of approach to solving problems, Osborn and Parnes, and is now well established so I shall use it (Osborn, 1957).

Figure 7. Structured CPS (based on the process of Dr. Min Basadur)

Broadly, the CPS process goes right from identifying the challenge (or problem), through idea generation and distillation, to the generation of a 'route map', all the way through the implementation of the solution. Whereas brainstorming might typically take one or two days, the whole CPS process will take substantially longer, and may be years for a complex challenge. As can be seen in Figure 4, some conceptualizations of CPS are circular since the implementation of a new process or product, or the solution of a particular problem, is seen by some to lead inevitably to the generation of new problems (or challenges).

In the original Osborn-Parnes model CPS is a six stage process, each of which incorporates both divergent and convergent thinking phases. My model adds to this in that I have team members conduct the divergent thinking phase individually. This helps make the CPS process compatible with the GAM. In other words, at each of the six stages, as in my brainstorming model, I have the group split up and individual team members go for a walk or go off on their own for 10-15 minutes. The convergent phase of each stage occurs when team members come back together and pool their ideas.

The CPS process, then, is as follows:

1. In a broad sense what is the goal of the current CPS session? In other words what is the challenge that it has been decided to tackle? At the corporate level this could be almost anything from 'How do we increase sales?' to 'How do we attract more skilled staff?'

    Sometimes this question or challenge is decided ahead of time, by the Board or upper management, perhaps. Alternatively this stage also comprises a brainstorming phase whereby team members generate ideas about what challenge they should be tackling in the subsequent CPS session.

    If you were to use this process as an individual coaching exercise, questions might look more like: 'What are your unfulfilled goals?' Or, 'What would you like to get out of life that you are not currently? And, once again, these questions could have been generated by an individual brainstorming session and were distilled from the idea generation process. So the applications for this kind of approach are broad.

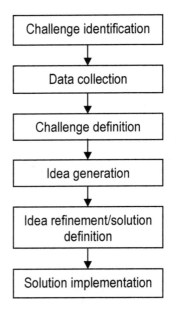

Figure 8: The six basic steps in CPS

2. In the *data collection* stage, team members (possibly with the help of those from outside the group) collect information that is pertinent to the goal or challenge. If our challenge from Stage 1 was 'How do we increase turnover?' then the kind of data to be collected at this stage

might include: What is the current level of domestic sales? What are our export sales? Do we have potential new products? Do we have the resources to develop new products? We might also find out what the industry norm is for domestic and export sales, to see how our current performance ranks against others, and what might be realistic future goals for each. Other information we might want to collect includes which territories we sell well into and where we sell very little.

When applied to the individual this data collection process would also depend very much on the challenges identified in Stage 1. For instance, the question: 'What are your unfulfilled goals?' might have yielded several answers, such as: 'To be a massage therapist'. The data collection stage might involve researching what qualifications are required to be a massage therapist in your geographic area, how long the training is, and how much it costs. You would probably do the same for the other results from Stage 1.

3. In Stage 3 our goal is to formulate the right question. Addressing our corporate challenge, 'How do we increase turnover?' we brief our CPS team with all the data collected regarding the answers from Stage 1 and then, as individuals, they set about generating ideas.

The data gathering exercise may have produced results suggesting that domestic sales are already above the industry norm but export sales are weak in most territories. It might be decided, then, that export sales represent the 'low fruit' and the specific challenge might become: 'How do we generate more export sales?'

Note that we have whittled the broad challenge down to a specific challenge through a combination of brainstorming and deductive processes. The Stage 1 brainstorming might have produced a large list of diverse results during the divergent phase. A shortlist would have been developed as a result of group conversation that might have included available resources, appropriate time frames, and other limiting factors. The collection and application of data may have caused the list to be refined further. Sometimes regulatory data will cause an idea to be eliminated because it is simply not legal to implement it.

Applying the process at the individual level is somewhat similar. Out of, say, seven unfulfilled goals the data collection stage may suggest that trying to fulfill five of these goals is impractical for one reason or another. Perhaps we conclude that we do not have the resources to drop everything and start training as a massage therapist;

perhaps some of the other goals are impractical for other reasons, or we simply feel the investment is too great.

4. Stage 4 is where brainstorming plays its principle and traditional role. We have a well-defined challenge and what we need now is ideas regarding how to tackle it. All the rules outlined previously regarding brainstorming need to be rigorously obeyed and the goal is simply to generate as many ideas as possible. Team members go away and individually generate their ideas for solving the identified challenge. When they return they share their ideas with all of the other team members. New ideas may well emerge from this process and this is to be encouraged. Plenty of time should be allotted for this stage. As mentioned previously, sometimes more than one individual divergent stage can be advantageous here so that the pooled ideas can be built on, first individually and then as a group.

5. Eventually, either the allotted time will have expired or the group will agree that the ideation process has been exhausted. Ideas can then be grouped with others that are similar and written onto large Post-its. They are stuck onto a large vertical surface (a wall, for instance) and arranged in a way that makes sense. If we were trying to improve our organization's public image, for instance, we might group *customer service* oriented ideas together. *Product quality* ideas might be grouped together on a different part of the wall, and *community relations* on yet another. It can sometimes be useful to increase the visualization of this stage by identifying different stakeholders and representing them visually, as in a Venn Diagram:

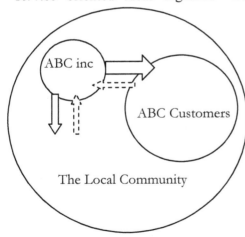

This diagram is representative of what can be brought up at the discussion (convergent) stage of the CPS process. Ideas may have been mentioned regarding communications and these lead to discussions about how

Figure 9. ABC Inc. delivers information well to its customers but doesn't 'listen' to them (hence the dotted line); similarly, with the local community.

effectively the organization communicates with all its stakeholders. Groups of Post-its can be attached to each other by arrows or strips of paper until everyone is satisfied that they are appropriately linked.

What often happens at this stage is that possible solutions are actually 'idea-sets' or groups of ideas that relate closely to each other. In other words possible solutions are identified that embrace the essence of several generated ideas that are similar. At that point the group needs to refine these idea-sets down to one manageable solution. The process is a satisfying one because it often generates an efficient answer: one whereby several smaller 'issues' are addressed at once.

6. The final stage is to draw up a route map regarding how the solution is to be achieved. This should be very detailed, specifically: Who does what? What is to be achieved by when? Who will organize the communication between team members? And; When and where will members next meet to discuss progress? The more detail in this section the better.

Often the implementation of the solution requires skills that are outside the capabilities of the brainstorming team so this stage needs to include details regarding how to gain access to those resources. If the web master needs to do some redesign of the corporate site, or a graphic artist needs to design a promotional piece, there may need to be a discussion regarding who authorizes that investment. Also those people external to the group who are involved in the solution may need to have access to critical information regarding their part in the solution process, so someone needs to be responsible for writing up the session. I generally photograph the Post-it note board as a useful start to this process, and also as an aid memoire for the next meeting.

Innovations are not always earth shattering and *revolutionary*; more often they are quite simple, relatively minor in their impact on the organization and the rest of the world, and *evolutionary* in nature. However, many small improvements in office efficiency or in manufacturing processes add up over time to a more efficient organization. If everyone within the organization becomes accustomed to the expectation that they perform creatively then major innovations will occur, if not immediately.

Chapter 9 – Creating the creative environment

'It is only when a society genuinely seeks to discover the talent
present in the population that we have a condition friendly
to the evocation of the creative urges...'

Melvin Tumin

In this chapter I will piece together characteristics that we might focus on in order to form the foundations of our creative organization. Every business is different, and profit-making companies will differ from non-profits; and, different leadership styles will tend to emphasize different possibilities in the stimulation of creativity. However, there are commonalities that we can draw from to help us generate our own models that we feel are best suited to our organizations and leadership styles.

The lone wolf

Although I am a firm believer that everyone has creative potential, I also believe that, as with other human characteristics, it is not distributed evenly among everyone. We particularly want to attract people into our organization who have appropriate skills and experience, and, importantly, that also have high creative potential. Abraham Maslow (of 'hierarchy of needs' fame) talks of the "lone wolf" nature of many creative people, and this "lone wolf" character may be the one we need.

> **A9.1 Can you identify a 'lone wolf' in an organization that you work for or are familiar with? Someone who has a reputation for doing things differently and is thought of as a bit of an anarchist (in the nicest possible way, of course!)**
>
> **Are that person's views treated with the same respect as the views or ideas of others?**

Since the beginning of the science of management, the lone wolf has presented a problem. The Taylorists, for instance, wanted uniformity and compliance, not the diversity and anarchy that is associated with the lone wolf. To some extent that philosophy is only now beginning to change. The creative people that we want to attract and keep in our innovative organization represent a challenge to the scientific management approach. Lone wolves have often tended to go and start their own businesses in order to avoid the constrictions that they perceive the corporate world would impose on them. We need to generate an environment that affords lone wolves the space necessary for their personal development and idea generation without the headaches associated with running their own organizations. We have to make sure that our constrictive influences are as few as possible, and we also have to let everyone know that this is one of our goals. In other words, a high degree of freedom and autonomy has to be incorporated into our organizational norms.

Simply emailing a memo saying *'starting immediately we are going to begin to value creativity and innovation'* simply isn't going to work! We need people within the organizational structure that will take ideas and values and run with them into the very core of the business. These people are our champions, and that role is often suited to the "lone wolf" that management theorists have had difficulty finding a role for. You all know champions, they take an idea and infect the whole establishment with it. That can be good or it can be bad, our job is to make sure we access the 'good' side of championing. We want our champion or champions to take our creative credo and help establish it throughout every vertical and horizontal area of the organization. In other words, the importance of our new values encouraging creativity and innovation needs to be championed and our lone wolf is just the one to do it.

Establishing an employee suggestion scheme is one way to get everyone focused on idea generation as a habit and may provide a way to spot our potential champions. They are the likely candidates for the frequent generation of new ideas and when they do we need to take them to one side and give them space and resources to develop them. When others see that happening the spreading of the word regarding the new corporate norm will have begun!

Mixing it up – the power of change

The more we can discourage schematic thinking the more innovative our organization will be. Decision making by using schemas is death to creativity, and schematic thinking is minimized by regular (but positive) changes to the environment. We don't want anyone's job to become humdrum - that just erodes motivation and is one step closer to 'clock-watching'. So, even when our corporate norms have been 'adjusted' to value innovative thought and action our commitment to change needs to continue. Creative people thrive on change so our lone-wolf/champion will be our ally here also.

Change is, of course, a double-edged sword. We want to create a dynamic environment where, to some extent, change is the norm, but we don't want to make the workplace uncomfortable. In the early days of Apple, there were people in Steve Jobs' organization who were not entirely happy with what they saw as his sometimes erratic behavior and decision making; but there is no doubt in my mind that it is one reason that Apple was so innovative.

The other advantage of a dynamic work environment is that it is inherently flexible; so, if changes are dictated by external forces such as the market in which it operates, or because the organization evolves in some way, they will be embraced more readily than by an organization that resists and does not see the value in change.

In the 1920s Western Electric commissioned a series of studies at their Hawthorne Works to see if workers' productivity changed in higher or lower levels of light. Researchers found that productivity seemed to improve when *any* of their changes occurred and then dropped to its previous level at the conclusion of the study. Although research into workplace lighting levels formed the basis of the studies, other changes such as relocating workstations, maintaining clean work stations and even keeping the floors clear of obstacles resulted in increased productivity for short periods. Thus the term Hawthorne Effect was coined in the 1950's by Henry A. Landsberger (Landsberger, 1958) and is used to identify any type of temporary productivity increase.

It was suggested that the productivity gain was due to a motivational effect of the interest being shown by the researchers in the electrical relay assembly workers. However, that has been criticized on several grounds including the fact that the conditions changed in so many different ways, including:

- the pay rules were changed so that the experimental group was not paid on an individual piece work basis (whereby each person was remunerated for her individual production) but on the basis of total group production.

- after discussion with the workers regarding the best length of time, they were given two 5-minute breaks. This was then changed to two 10-minute breaks. This was not their preference, however, but productivity still increased. But when they received six 5-minute rests, they disliked it and output fell.

- reducing the length of the working day by 30 minutes increased output. However, shortening it further reduced overall output although output per hour still increased. Then returning to the first condition caused the productivity to peak!

- providing food during the breaks increased productivity.

Interviewing the test group did reveal that the workers appreciated being listened to and having some 'say' regarding their working conditions. It is rather surprising that, in general, managerial practices did not react to this finding that upward communication through organizations has such a positive potential to influence productivity and employee well-being.

One other explanation regarding the Hawthorne Effect is not so much that people increase productivity when they think they are being observed (the experiments continued for eight years so the participants probably got used to that condition), but that people simply embrace any kind of change, especially when their jobs are particularly monotonous (as the relay assemblers' undoubtedly were).

Change is likely to have positive repercussions for the work environment that we are creating, aside from promoting creative, non-schematic decision making.

Freedom of expression

A couple of years ago I read about a Silicon Valley business that let its employees do anything they liked with their office spaces. One guy built a bunk bed above his desk! I'm not sure whether he did all-nighters from time to time or he just needed to nap but I feel sure he felt a strong sense of his own identity, in being allowed, encouraged in fact, to express himself in this way.

A9.2 In what ways could rules be relaxed or individuality be given more opportunity for expression in your organization (or an organization with which you are familiar?)

For today's lean, mean, money making machines, excess office space is scarce, but if you have a spare room why not create a games area? We all need to take breaks and a game of darts, foosball or cards might be just the thing to give your mind a rest from the problem in hand (remember, fun is conducive to creativity). Flexibility regarding when we take breaks might be a good idea also. The Wimbledon or US Open enthusiast might appreciate being able to take lunch at 10 a.m. if that's when the big match is on. In other words, we need to decide what are the critical constraints in our corporate structure, and which ones really don't matter that much, and consider eliminating those we conclude are unnecessary.

Below you can read a brief company profile of one of Britain's most successful empires, that of maverick Richard Branson's Virgin Group. Virgin was founded 40 years ago and now has an annual turnover of the

---

Virgin Group: A Brief Profile

Virgin Group is one of the U.K.'s largest business empires, with businesses in travel, telecommunications, financial services, leisure, cosmetics, retail, and music. The company's fundamental values foster many of the dimensions of its organizational culture, and Virgin's founder, Richard Branson, who realizes the potential and importance of those who work for him, and created a decentralized structure which empowers employees. The structure of the Virgin Group is such that there is little bureaucracy and Branson encourages employees to use their intuition to make decisions rather than rational thinking processes. Each of Virgin's 200 subsidiaries operates as an autonomous entity under Branson's ownership or as a minority or majority shareholder. In other words the Virgin Group identity does not dominate as a strong corporate presence within the empire.

Branson's philosophy is that "if you keep your staff happy then the customer will be happy, and if you keep the customer happy then the shareholders are happy". This fundamental tenet underlies the corporate culture of each Virgin company. From casual dress code to acceptance of personal responsibility and working long hours when needed, this philosophy has enabled Branson to create a casual, non-corporate work environment, which is continuously redefined by the pop culture of its era. This work climate encourages positive vertical communication and demonstrates the importance of positive interpersonal relations. Emphasizing the value of communication within his empire, Branson established an internal virtual community, The Virgin Village, the function of which is to ensure that all Virgin employees get a 'bird's-eye' view of the group as a whole. The site gives employees access to information about the company, job opportunities, contacts, and other information.

Human resources are viewed as Virgin's greatest asset and as such, management believes that they should be treated with respect by allowing them the freedom to flourish and be themselves. Virgin actively encourages personal expression, whether it is though speech, creative and conceptual thinking, or dress. According to Branson, the key to encouraging innovation within the company is to listen to ideas and to offer feedback; so, once again, intra-organizational communications are a vital part of the Virgin equation.

order of $20 billion with business interests from passenger trains and airplanes to telecommunications, entertainment and cosmetics.

Virgin is living proof that businesses built on a flat decision making structure, with plenty of room for employee autonomy can grow and be extremely successful. A casual dress code, a charismatic leader, self expression and risk-taking as part of the corporate norm, are not merely of academic interest at Virgin, they are at the core of its business model and its success.

O'Reilly et al. identified seven dimensions of organizational culture (1991). Three dimensions relate to how tasks are conducted; they are *detail*, *stability*, and *innovation*. Two more dimensions refer to values regarding interpersonal relations; they are *respect for people*, and *team orientation*. The final two dimensions are *outcome orientation*, which refers to performance expectations, and *aggressiveness* which refers to the corporate norm regarding competition. Virgin Group appears to emphasize three of these dimensions in particular: *aggressiveness*, *innovation*, and *respect for people*.

Aggressiveness is very evident in Virgin's culture since it has taken opportunities ahead of the competition, sometimes at the expense of larger and more cumbersome corporations. It is also evident that Virgin focuses on innovation. One expression of this is their keenness to offer better and more valuable products to their customers. Another sign that Virgin values innovation is the 'flat' nature of its organizational structure (Damanpour, 1996). Innovation and the associated risk-taking have been crucial to Virgin's success.

As well as innovativeness, another factor associated with flat organizations, such as Virgin, is effective communication channels and good intra-organizational coordination. Both of these contribute to faster and more efficient decision making. Also, a flatter organizational structure with a broad based DMS results in employees enjoying a wider range of responsibilities. This promotes a sense of autonomy, employee empowerment and satisfaction.

Virgin Group is one example of how visionary leadership, willingness to take risks, and respect for employees *and* for their potential, can generate huge successes. Richard Branson did not, I feel sure, sit down and read books like this before he formed his first company, but we are not all blessed with his intuitive insight regarding leadership, opportunity and innovation. All we can do instead is to try and learn retrospectively from this and other examples. In doing so I believe we should strive to establish an environment where:

- people feel encouraged to identify challenges and generate ideas for new products, markets and ways of doing things.

- risk taking is part of the organizational norm.

- red-tape is minimized.

- it is OK to make mistakes.

- challenging goals are set.

- people feel safe and unthreatened by intra-organizational factors.

- the demonstration of individuality is supported and some degree of anarchy is at least tolerated.

- innovation is positively rewarded. The reward may be partly extrinsic but mainly intrinsic – i.e. a good idea can be rewarded by the opportunity to lead a team to pursue the idea further.

The outcome should be an organization that is flexible and able to adapt to conditions of calm or turbulence. With businesses that are run on a day to day basis by innovative and empowered teams their leaders will have the time and support to seek out opportunities that hide within the peaks and troughs of turbulence and calm. An innovative and empowered company is a coordinated team of individuals focused on the future and not the past, who take decisive control and act on it. Not all such teams will be successful, but increasingly in the competitive future, successful organizations will be teams such as this.

In closing let us revisit Federico Fellini and try to live, or at least think, spherically and let us embrace the era of creativity!

References

Ajzen, I., & Fishbein, M. (1980). *Understanding attitudes and predicting social behavior.* Englewood Cliffs, NJ: Prentice Hall.

Amabile, T. M. (1983). *The social psychology of creativity.* New York: Springer-Verlag.

Amabile, T. M., Goldfarb, P., & Brackfield, S. C. (1990). Social influences on creativity: Evaluation, coaction, and surveillance. *Creativity Research Journal, 3,* 6–21.

Arndt, J., Greenberg, J., & Cook, A. (2002). Mortality salience and the spreading activation of worldview-relevant constructs: Exploring the cognitive architecture of terror management. *Journal of Experimental Psychology, 131,* 307-324.

Arndt, J., Greenberg, J., Pyszczynski, T., Solomon, S., & Schimel, J. (1999). Creativity and Terror management: Evidence that creative activity increases guilt and social projection following mortality salience. *Journal of Personality and Social Psychology, 77,* 19-31.

Autio, E. (2007). *GEM 2007 report on high-growth entrepreneurship.* London: Global Entrepreneurship Research Association.

Baer, J. R. (1998). Gender differences in the effects of extrinsic motivation. *Journal of Creative Behavior, 32,* 18–37.

Basadur, M. S., & Gelade, G. (2002). Knowing and thinking: A new theory of creativity. *Management of Innovation and New Technology Research Centre Working Paper 105.*

Basadur, M. S., & Head, M. (2001). Team performance and satisfaction: A link to cognitive style within a process framework. *Journal of Creative Behavior, 35,* 1-22.

Bass, B. M. (1985). *Leadership and performance beyond expectation.* New York: Free Press.

Bass, B. M., & Avolio, B. J. (1993). Transformational leadership: A response to critiques. In M. Chemmers, & R. Ayman (Eds.), *Leadership: Perspectives and research directions,* (pp. 49-80). New York: Academic Press.

Baumeister, R. F., & Leary, M. R. (1995). The need to belong: Desire for interpersonal attachments as a fundamental human motivation. *Psychological Bulletin, 177,* 497-529.

Becker, E. (1973). *The denial of death.* New York: Free Press.

Bhawuk, D. P. (2003). Culture's influence on creativity: The case of Indian spirituality. *International Journal of Intercultural Relations, 27,* 1-22

Branscombe, N. R., & Wann, D. L. (1994). Collective self-esteem consequences of outgroup derogation when a valued social identity is on trial. *European Journal of Social Psychology, 24,* 641-657.

Branscombe, N. R., Ellemers, N., Spears, R., & Doosje, B. (1999). The context and content of social identity threat. In N. Ellemers, & R. Spears (Eds.), *Social identity: Context, commitment, content,* (pp. 35-58). Oxford: Blackwell.

Branscombe, N. R., Wann, D. L., Noel, J. G., & Coleman, J. (1993). In-group or out-group extremity: Importance of the threatened social identity. *Personality & Social Psychology Bulletin, 19,* 381-388.

Bunce, D., & West, M. A. (1995). Changing work environments: Innovative coping responses to occupational stress. *Work and Stress, 8*, 319-331.

Byron, K., Khazanchi, S., & Nazarian, D. (2010). The relationship between stressors and creativity: A meta-analysis examining competing theoretical models. *Journal of Applied Psychology, 95*, 201-212.

Claxton, G. L. (1997). *Have brain, tortoise mind: Why intellignece increases when you think less.* London: Fourth Issue.

Claxton, G. L. (1998). Knowing without Knowing why: Investigating human intuition. *The Psychologist, 11*, 217-220.

Clark, D. M., & Teasdale, J. D. (1985). Constraints of the effects of mood. *Journal of Personality and Social Psychology, 48*, 1595–1608.

Coren, S., & Schulman, M. (1971). Effects of an external stress on a commonality of verbal associates. *Psychological Reports, 28*, 328-330.

Damanpour, F. (1996). Organizational complexity and innovation: Developing and testing multiple contingency models. *Management Science, 42*, 693-717.

Damasio, A. R. (1994). *Descarte's error: Emotion, reason and the human brain.* New York: Putnam.

Deci, E. L., & Ryan, R. M. (1985). *Intrinsic motivation and self determination.* New York: Plenum.

Diehl, M., & Stroebe, W. (1987). Productivity loss in brainstorming groups: Tracking down the blocking effect. *Journal of Personality and Social Psychology, 53*, 497-509.

Dijksterhuis, A. (2004). Think different: The merits of unconscious thought in preference development and decision making. *Journal of Personality and Social Psychology, 85*, 586-598.

Dollinger, S. J., Palaskonis, D. G., & Pearson, J. L. (2004). Creativity and intuition revisited. *Journal of Creative Behavior, 38*, 244-259 .

Eisenberger, R., & Rhoades, L. (2001). Incremental effects of reward on creativity. *Journal of Personality and Social Psychology, 81*, 728-741.

Euchner, J. A. (2010). Managing in turbulent times. *Research Technology Management, 53*, 9-10.

Fishbein, M. (1967). Attitude and the prediction of behavior. In M. Fishbein (Ed.), *Readings in attitude theory and measurement* (pp. 477-492). New York: Wiley.

Fishbein, M., & Ajzen, I. (1975). *Belief, attitude, intention, and behavior: An introduction to theory and research.* Reading, MA: Addison-Wesley.

Galin, D. (1974). Implications for psychiatry of left and right cerebral specializations: A neurophysiological context for unconscious processes. *Archives of General Psychiatry, 31*, 572-583.

Gardner, H. (1983). *Frames of mind.* New York: Basic Books.

Gouldner, A. (1957). Cosmopolitans and locals: toward an analysis of latent social roles. *Administrative Science Quarterly, 2*, 281-306.

Guilford, J. P. (1967). *The nature of human intelligence.* New York: McGraw-Hill.

Hersey, P., & Blanchard, K. H. (1972). *Management of Organizational Behavior: Utilizing Human Resources (2nd ed.).* New Jersey: Prentice Hall.

Hoppe, K. (1977). Brains and psychoanalysis. *Psychoanalytic Quarterly*, 220-224.

Horton, D. L., Marlow, D., & Crowne, D. (1963). The effect of instructional set and need for social approval on commonality of word association responses. *Journal of Abnormal and Social Psychology, 66*, 67-72.

Jetten, J., Postmes, T., & McAuliffe, B. J. (2002). 'We're all individuals': group norms of individualism and collectivism, levels of identification and identity threat. *European Journal of Social Psychology, 32*, 189-297.

Kirton, M.J. (2004). *Adaption-Innovation In the Context of Diversity and Change.* Oxford: Routledge

Kris, E. (1952). *Psychoanalytic explorations in art.* New York: International Universities Press.

Landon, P. B., & Suedfeld, P. (1972). Complex cognitive performance. *Perceptual and Motor, 34*, 601–602.

Landsberger, H. A. (1958). *Hawthorne Revisited.* New York: Ithaca.

Levitin, D. J. (2006). *This is your brain on music.* New York: Dutton/Penguin.

Martindale, C. (1999). Biological bases of creativity. In R. J. Sternberg (Ed.), *Handbook of creativity* (pp. 137-152). New York, NY: Cambridge University Press.

Maslow, A. H. (1968). *Toward a psychology of being.* New York: Van Nostrand.

Mayer, J. D., & Salovey, P. (1997). What is emotional intelligence? In P. Salovey, & D. J. Sluyter (Eds.), *Emotional development and emotional intelligence: Educational implications* (pp. 3-34). New York, NY: Basic Books.

Meisels, M. (1967). Test anxiety, stress and verbal behavior. *Journal of Consulting Psyhchology, 31*, 577-582.

Moskalenko, S., McCauley, C., & Rozin, P. (2006). Group identification under conditions of threat: College students' attachment to country, family, ethnicity, religion, and university before and after September 11, 2001. *Political Psychology, 27*, 77-97.

Myers, I. B. (1998). *Introduction to type, 6th ed.*, L. K. Kirby & K. D. Myers (eds.). Palo Alto, CA: Consulting Psychologists Press

Oke, A., Munshi, N., & Walumbwa, F. (2009). The Influence of Leadership on Innovation Processes and Activities. *Organizational Dynamics, 38*, 64-72.

O'Reilly, C. A., Chatman, J., & Caldwell, D. F. (1991). People and organizational culture: A profile comparison approach to assessing person-organization fit. *Academy of Management Journal, 34*, 487-516.

Osborn, A. F. (1957). *Applied imagination.* New York: Schribner.

Osgood, C. E. (1960). Some effects of motivation on style on encoding. In T. Sebeok (Eds.), *Style in language* (pp. 293-306). Cambridge, MA: MIT Press.

Paulus, P. B., & Nijstad, B. A. (2003). Group creativity: An introduction. In P. B. Paulus, B. A. Nijstad (Eds.), *Group creativity: Innovation through collaboration* (pp. 3-11). New York, NY: Oxford University Press.

Paulus, P. B., Dzindolet, M. T., Poletes, G., & Camacho, L. M. (1993). Perception of performance in group brainstorming: The illusion of group productivity. *Personality & Social Psychology Bulletin, 19*, 78-89.

Perkins, D. (1981). *The mind's best work.* Cambridge, MA: Harvard University Press.

Petrides, K. V., Pita, R., & Kokkinaki, F. (2007). The location of trait emotional intelligence in personality factor space. *British Journal of Psychology, 40*, 273-289.

Rank, O. (1932/1989). *Art and artist: Creative urge and personality development.* New York: Knopf.

Rogers, C. (1954). Towards a theory of creativity. *ETC: A review of general semantics, 11*, 249-260.

Tajfel, H. (1981). *Human groups and social categories.* Cambridge, U.K: Cambridge University Press.

Tajfel, H., & Turner, J. C. (1986). The social identity theory of intergroup behavior. In S. W. Austin (Ed.), *Psychology of intergroup relation* (pp. 7-24). Chicago: Nelson Hall.

Thorndike, R. K. (1920). Intelligence and its uses. *Harper's Magazine, 140*, 227-335.

Torrance, E. P. (1962). *Guiding creative talent.* Engelwood Cliffs, NJ: Prentice Hall.

Torrance, E. P. (1974). *Torrance Tests of Creative Thinking: Norms-technical manual.* Princeton, NJ: Personnel Press/Ginn.

Tsang, D. (2002). *Business strategy and national culture.* Northampton, MA: Edward Elgar Publishing

Walton, A. P. (2006). Social influences on creativity: Threat, group affiliation, and norms. *Dissertation Abstracts International: Section B: The Sciences and Engineering, 67, 1-B*, 604.

Wechsler, D. (1958). *The measurement and appraisal of adult intelligence (4th ed.).* Baltimore, MD: Williams & Wilkins.

Wechsler, D. (1941). *The measurement of adult intelligence (2nd ed.).* Baltimore, MD: Williams & Wilkins.

Westcott, M. R. (1968). *Toward a Contemporary Psychology of Intuition: A Historical, Theoretical, and Empirical Inquiry.* New York: Holt, Rinehart & Winston

West, M. A. (1989). Innovation among healthcare professionals. *Social Behavior, 4*, 173-184.

West, M. A., & Sacramento, C. A. (2006). Flourishing in teams: developing creativity and innovation. In J. Henry (Ed.), *Creative Management and Development (3rd ed.)* (pp. 25-44). Thousand Oaks, CA: Sage.

Wilson, T. D., & Schooler, J. W. (1991). Thinking too much: Introspection can reduce the quality of preferences and decisions. *Journal of Personality and Social Psychology, 60*, 181-192.

Wilson, T. D., Dunn, D. S., Kraft, D., & Lisle, D. J. (1989). Introspection, attitude change, and attitude– behavior consistency: The disruptive effects of explaining why we feel the way we do. In L. Berkowitz (Ed.), *Advances in Experimental Social Psychology, 19*, 123-205. Orlando, FL: Academic Press.

Wright, T. A., & Staw, B. M. (1999). Affect and favorable work outcomes: Two longitudinal tests of the happyproductive. *Journal of Organizational Behavior, 20*, 1-23.

Wright, T. A., & Walton, A. P. (2003). Affect, psychological well-being and creativity: Results of a field study. *Journal of Business and Management*, 21-32.

Yamamoto, K. (1964). Threshold of intelligence in academic achievement of highly creative students. *Journal of Experimental Education, 32*, 401–405.

Zahra, S. A., Filatotchev, I., & Wright, M. (2009). How do threshold firms sustain corporate entrepreneurship? The role of boards and absorptive capacity. *Journal of Business Venturing, 24*, 248-260.

Zajonc, R. (1965). Social facilitation. *Science, 149*, 269-274.

CPSIA information can be obtained
at www.ICGtesting.com
Printed in the USA
FSHW022034220321
79767FS